The
ENGLISH DRAMA

The ENGLISH DRAMA

edited by

K.S. IYER
PRADIP R. PATIL
M.B. KAUTHEKAR

PRESTIGE

in association with

Tuljaram Chaturchand College, Baramati

Published by
PRESTIGE BOOKS
3/28, East Patel Nagar
New Delhi 110 008

2000

ISBN: 81-7551-080-3

Composed by Vivek Mathur, Delhi 110 006 Ph. 3981867
Printed by Dhawan Industries Offset, New Delhi 110 028

Contents

The Restoration Drama

The Social Drama

The Absurd Drama

The Modern Drama

Contributors

N.M. ASTON	Reader and Head Nowrosjee Wadia College, Pune
MANOJ BHISE	Reader, Nowrosjee Wadia College Pune
SUNANDA CHAVAN	Reader and Head C.S. College, Satara
NISHI CHAWLA	Gargi College University of Delhi
A.P. DANI	Reader and Head Fergusson College, Pune
SHARAD GADEKAR	Head, Arts and Science College Varvand
SHILPAGAURI GANPULE	A.C.S. College Akurdi
MADHURI S. GOKHALE	Department of English University of Pune
SRIDHAR B. GOKHALE	Reader, Department of English University of Pune
B.N. KULKARNI	Principal, Sir Parashurambhau College, Pune (Since Retd.)
V.M. MADGE	Reader and Head Waghire College, Saswad
CASHMERE MAINDARKAR	Nowrosjee Wadia College Pune
PRABHANJAN MANE	T.C. College Baramati
JANARDHAN NAIR	C.T. Bora College Shirur
K. VENKATA REDDY	Sri Krishnadevaraya University Anantapur
PRABHA SAMPATH	St. Mira's College Pune
JAYAPRAKASH SHINDE	Reader, Shivaji University Kolhapur
PRASHANT K. SINHA	Professor and Head University of Pune

Introduction

The evolution of English drama can be broadly categorized as passing through several stages of ups and downs. The earliest of the stages can be taken to be that from Miracle plays to Marlowe. The second phase is the acme drama attained during Shakespeare's writing career. The third phase can be reckoned as the period from Ben Jonson's comedies to the closing of the theatres under Oliver Cromwell's Protectorate. The fourth phase saw the return of Monarchy in England with the outburst of comic vein in drama oscillating between the efforts to elevate the comedy as high comedy and at the other extreme comedy deteriorated into glorification of social behaviour and promiscuity of every kind and shade. The fifth phase saw the re-emergence of comedy at the hands of Oliver Goldsmith and Sheridan as a frontal attack on eighteenth century sentimentalism and the reinstatement of high comedy. The sixth phase began with Wilde's *The Importance of Being Earnest*, nearly one hundred years after Sheridan's comedies extending as far as Shaw's problem comedies. Comedy as a Mode of Being reached a high watermark with social questions coming within its ambit.

Shaw and Galsworthy and other lesser lights held sway over minds of audiences for a quarter century or so. With the two World Wars unleashing several, erstwhile unthought of human questions, a wave of existentialist and absurdist plays with Beckett, Genet, Ionesco, Pinter and others as their exponents, swept across the European Continent focusing serious attention on the immediacy and essentiality of ameliorating by uplifting human life from the predicament of being condemned to live in a godless world. This was the seventh phase in the evolution of drama as a reflection of a mode of being.

The eighth phase, an off-shoot of the disillusionment with the Ideology of the Welfare State in European democracies, put up a series of plays coming under the banner of Angry Theatre and the plays of the type of Robert Bolt's *A Man for All Seasons* exploring the concept of selfhood by reviving and reinterpreting past history. A third off-shoot of this phase was the revival of interest in poetic drama with Eliot's *Murder in the Cathedral.*

It has been the endeavour of the editors to include in this volume, articles on plays falling in and representative of, each of the aforesaid phases. We have met with some success, though not total success. The plays dealt with do broadly connect contemporary drama with the earliest, as we have plays in this volume from Faustus to Pinter, with an exhaustive, bird's eye-view of the evolution of the Absurd Theatre presented by Prashant Sinha's article.

II

Janardhan Nair's article, "Where Shall Faustus Flee: A Study of Christopher Marlowe's *Dr. Faustus*" is an attempt at a new reading of *Dr. Faustus* in relation to the concept of 'selfhood.' Nair examines how the play registers the different movements of Faustus till he confronts selfhood and realizes to his consternation that he had lost his 'self' and had nowhere to flee, but to face damnation.

In her article "Darkness in Shakespearean Tragedy with Special Reference to *Macbeth*," Cashmere Maindarkar focuses on the symbolic darkness in Lear's mind and in his elder daughters's hearts; in *Hamlet* the darkness appears with the visitation of the ghost and in Claudius's dark deeds; in *Othello* it is the darkness caused by Othello's jealousy; in *Macbeth* it is symbolized by Macbeth's deeds and the witches's prophecies. Cashmere argues that darkness represents the evil forces which are ultimately overpowered and dispelled by moral order having been reinstated.

Madhuri Gokhale's article, entitled "Songs in Shakespeare's *King Lear*," examines the function of songs in *King Lear* focusing on their uniqueness. Gokhale categorizes the songs as 'the called-for' and 'impromptu' songs, and argues that these work a therapeutic effect on the psychological and physical suffering of Lear, as well as yield a phonic pleasure to the spectators. She emphasizes the significance of the Fool's songs which, as the play progresses, bring about gradual salubrious effect on Lear.

N.M. Aston's article, entitled "Imagery in Shakespeare's *Macbeth*: A Study" highlights the rich, varied and largely imaginative images employed by Shakespeare in *Macbeth*. Aston particularizes the imagery relating to 'dress,' 'robe' etc. which signify Macbeth's predicament after he murders Duncan, illustrating copiously from the text.

Prabha Sampath, in her scintillating paper, "Love, Marriage and the Status of Women in Shakespeare's *The Taming of the Shrew*," coinciding with the Women's Day—8th March 1997—while cautioning readers against the delusion of believing Shakespeare to be a feminist, argues that the play projects the Elizabethan attitude to love, marriage and women and nothing more and nothing less. Sampath considers that the play is the "only Shakespearean comedy in which the woman is re-educated; in all the rest it is the man."

In his article "Profit and Delight: The Plays of Ben Jonson," K. Venkata Reddy brings out the didactic and aesthetic elements in Jonson's comedies while maintaining that Jonson is not a conventional moralist, but essentially a comic dramatist using the didactic theory for literary and dramatic purposes

Sharad Gadekar, in his article "Sheridan's *The School for Scandal* as High Comedy," traces the development of the genre of high comedy from Shakespeare, Moliere, the Restoration Period, Sheridan to Wilde and Shaw to show that it has survived and sustained itself through its prevailing wit and the equality of men and women. Gadekar considers Sheridan's play as a forerunner of modern high comedy as it stands midway between two states of its development and perfection.

Shilpagauri Ganpule's article on "The Proviso Scene in William Congreve's *The Way of the World*" examines the significance of the scene apropos of contemporary attitude towards love and marriage. She argues that the scene is a reflection of the rationality behind marriage namely, a relationship based on mutual understanding, serving as a prelude to a future happy, married life. It foregrounds the true identity of the parties to the Bargain.

A.P. Dani, in his article "G.B. Shaw's *The Doctor's Dilemma*:

A Problem Play," argues that Shaw has not succeeded in projecting his thesis that 'though art is ennobling, the artist may be ignoble,' due to his failure to focus convincingly on the artist, Dubedat's genius. Dani thinks that Shaw's ambivalence regarding his approval of a good man against a scoundrel with creative powers, bypasses the solution to the problem which he raises in the course of the play.

B.N. Kulkarni, in his article "Naturalism and Beyond: The Poetic Element in John Galsworthy's Plays," succinctly presents his arguments to establish the inherent poetic strength of Galsworthy, as evidenced in his plays such as *The Silver Box, Strife* and *Justice* and *A Little Dream, Joy* and *A Bit O'Love* falling into two groups dealing with social and economic problems and exploration of human relationships against the backdrop of nature, respectively. Kulkarni convincingly argues that Galsworthy, despite being an exponent of naturalism, goes beyond, to permeate his plays with poetry, thereby enriching his plays.

In his masterly article on "The Theatre of the Absurd," Prashant Sinha argues at the outset that elements of the absurd had been present in plays and novels much before Martin Esslin familiarized readers with his coinage of the term. Sinha goes back to Shakespeare's *King Lear*, and arrives at Chekhov's *The Three Sisters,* Maeterlinck's *The Intruder,* Strindberg's *The Ghost Sonata,* Pirandello's *Six Characters in Search of an Author* and Kafka's *The Trial* to show that absurdist elements such as lack of a moral scheme and meaning in the world, failure of communication, irrationality, purposelessness had been handled earlier as well. Later writers like Camus, Sartre, Genet, Beckett, Pinter, and Stoppard helped the absurd theatre to emerge as a truthful depiction of the contemporary world after the Second World War.

Foucault's historicizing of power, knowledge and theatricality in his *Discipline and Punish* engages with a form of tyranny and bodily repression that can be closely applied to the play of power relations found in Beckett's writings. In her article "The Body's Disciplining," Nishi Chawla applies the Foucauldian paradigm to Samuel Beckett's *Waiting for Godot*

Manoj Bhise, in his article "Samuel Beckett's *Endgame*: A Game That Never Ends," conducts an in-depth analysis of the play.

He considers the play as evocative of a ritual of agony in relation to the impending end of civilisation. Commenting on 'language' in the play, he defends the play as projecting an expression beyond what language can do. The article concludes with the inevitability of the 'game' of life never ending and with the insinuation that pain and suffering are a continuum.

Shridhar B. Gokhale in his article, "The Speech Act Theory and the Analysis of Drama," emphasizes the role of speech acts in the dynamics of drama, by illustrating the usefulness and limitation as well, of the study of speech acts with reference to Beckett's *Waiting for Godot*. Gokhale contends that the play—in the several instances adduced—presents a 'rupture' of communication, thereby limiting the application of Speech Act theory to such a play as Beckett's,

Prabhanjan Mane, in his article "Recurrent Motifs in Harold Pinter's *The Room, The Dumb Waiter* and *The Birthday Party*," argues that *The Birthday Party* is a curious mixture of Pinter's One-Act plays, *The Room* and *The Dumb Waiter*. Mane points out that certain motifs such as menace, the door, the intruder, the hired killers etc. of the two one-act plays recur in *The Birthday Party* which are only the reflections of the terror and insecurity we face in the world.

V.M. Madge, in his article entitled, "'A Play is a Play, is a Play': T.S. Eliot's *Murder in the Cathedral*" provides a rejoinder to questions relating to the play raised at a workshop for undergraduates by two paper-readers. The arguments advanced were: (a) Eliot's political opinions were reactionary and that the play was anti-democratic in spirit; (b) Eliot's play was an instance of 'Christian apologetics,' (c) that the play was a distortion of history, since it is 'selective.' Madge refutes the contentions of the paper-readers by arguing that (a) Eliot's play was a poetic drama examining deeply the question of Becket's sainthood; and (b) that art is selection.

In his article entitled "John Osborne's *Look Back in Anger*: A Critique of the Welfare State," Jayaprakash Shinde focuses on Jimmy Porter, the hero, the Angry Young Man, who is disillusioned with the Welfare State which failed to offer him a life suiting his talents. Needless to say, the only antidote to a failed-life, thanks to the Welfare State, is to have recourse to the world of fantasy, argues Shinde.

Sunanda P. Chavan, in her article, "*A Man for All Seasons* as Robert Bolt's Diagnosis of Modern Man's Malady" examines the place of man in modern society. She argues succinctly, substantiating evidences from the text to show that modern man's tragedy is, ironically enough, his inability to stand up heroically for selfhood. The paper stresses the essentiality of man to uphold his private conscience even in matters of state. More's tragedy, she points out, is due to the defeat of the very concept of a Welfare State, in which private conscience is sacrificed to public duties, with the ultimate consequence of chaos in the country.

III

We have no words to express our gratitude to Dr. R.K. Dhawan of Delhi University who has been instrumental in making it possible for us to bring out a second book—this, on English Drama—within a space of three months. We are grateful to the Management of the College—The Anekant Education Society, Baramati—and more particularly to M.M. Gandhi for providing us with funds to bring out two books in quick succession. Our sincere thanks are due to Dr. Prashant K. Sinha, Professor and Head, Department of English, University of Pune for his suggestion that we bring out a book on English Drama as well as his valuable advice from time to time. We are also thankful to all the contributors for their readiness in contributing their articles. We sincerely record our appreciation of the work done by Prestige Books—the quality of printing, designing of cover and the in-set.

Where Shall Faustus Flee?: A Study of Christopher Marlowe's *Dr. Faustus*

JANARDHAN NAIR

> The concept of the substance is a consequence of the concept of the subject: not the reverse. If we relinquish the soul, "the subject" the precondition for "substance" in general disappears. One acquires degrees of being, one loses that which 'has' being.
>
> Nietzsche

Writing towards the end of his life, in his introduction to *The History of Sexuality*, Foucault comes up with a rhetorical question. The question, which reverberates throughout his intellectual career in different forms, has a certain theoretical primacy in that it asks after the very nature of thinking. Foucault asks: "But, what then, is philosophy today—philosophical activity, I mean—if it is not the critical work that thought brings to bear on itself? In what does it consist, if not in the endeavour to know how and to what extent it might be possible to think differently, instead of legitimating what is already known?"[1]

Foucault's influence on literary criticism in the English speaking world, particularly in relation to the reading of Renaissance literary text, is a factor too well known to be demonstrated here at any length. Admittedly, this paper is also inspired by the various readings of different Renaissance texts under the influence of contemporary literary theory, particularly the writings of Foucault and hence it may fail at times to pay "the deserving degree of attention" to some of the conventional norms of literary criticism. Further, the paper might even be lacking in providing a lot of empirical evidences to substantiate some of its theoretical assumptions. However, such anxieties, valid though they are, I feel, should not discourage one from attempting an alternative reading of the text under consideration, from asking as to what extent it might be possible to think differently of *Doctor Faustus* instead of legitimating what is already known (about the play). And hence we start our reading by positing a fundamental though not a very fashionable question.

The question in relation to which a large number of issues in contemporary literary criticism can be discussed is—how does one equally understand and appreciate tragedies of different ages of different cultures? A "commonsensical" answer to this vaguely put question, as it is implied in several theories of tragedy is that, irrespective of their socio-cultural, historical and religious differences, tragedies portray human beings in distress and hence they have a universal appeal. This "commonsensical" view of tragedy, often uncritically accepted and untimely applied, has several theoretical implications which are to be seriously analyzed. Among other less obvious assumptions, it implies that beyond the socio-historical variations (which in this view are merely superficial), human life involves a certain essential suffering. Consequently, this view would compel us to believe that man in distress, be it Oedipus or Lear, Kafka's K or a "tragic" character in a pulp novel or formula movie, is essentially the same in that despite its contextual variations, suffering has a certain universal essence. "Tragic man" in this view appears as the exemplary depiction of the absolute human potential and the unchangeable human predicament, which includes a certain essential suffering. But it should be noted that the view, which attributes a certain unchanging essence to human suffering and treats suffering as an essential human predicament also, by extension attributes a similar unchanging essence to the human self.

In fact this ontological notion of the human self is not limited to certain theories of tragedy alone. A theoretical reading of the history of literary criticism would reveal that this notion of the ontology of the human self, transcending its historical variations, is widely operational in a large number of constitutive notions underlying Western literature and literary criticism. It seems to serve as basic principle that helps establish similarities and connections and often a sense of unbroken continuity between men of different socio-cultural and historical milieus. A theory of literature based on such an implicit assumption of the human self enables one to read literatures of all times and of different socio-political and religious milieus as if they were timeless portrayals of a certain unchanging human essence—the Eternal Man. This is what Bertolt Brecht half-humorously says about the Eternal Man of the Western Capitalistic world.

> Man with capital M drinks coffee every afternoon, is jealous of his wife, wants to get on in this world, and only more or less manages to: more often less. 'People don't change much,' he says, and if he himself is less agreeable to his wife than he was twenty years ago, it's just that men have always been less agreeable to their wives at forty-five than at twenty-five. 'Love is timeless,' he says, and would sooner have no idea about the term's original meaning and the practices covered by it.[2]

Literary criticism in the liberal humanist tradition seems to have understood tragedy as the expression of a certain (unchanging and inevitable) human experience. If this view is granted, literary history, by extension, should have been a history of experience. But if no such claim was made in relation to literary history, it is primarily because experience was understood to be transparent to itself. Any attempt at an alternative reading of *Doctor Faustus* has to begin by exposing these conventional assumptions primarily because a major bulk of existing Marlowe criticism seems to endorse the liberal humanist notion of the human self. It is also true that many of those who practise traditional schools of criticism feel uncomfortable with the emerging trends and lament the loss of the values cherished by the humanist tradition. The anxiety expressed by Robert Watson in an influential book written in 1990 could bear testimony to the general concern of a very large number of critics in the Anglo-American literary critical tradition who insist on the virtues of clarity, continuity and commonsense. Watson complains:

"Contemporary criticism has an unfortunate tendency to construct artificial barriers between past and present, to scold modern student of attempting to experience Renaissance tragedies as accessible expressions of precious if painful insights."[3] Further Watson attempts to develop an essentialist view of tragedy by tracing its trans-historical edge. He writes:

> Tragedy typically reminds its audience of something they share and commonly struggle to forget: the progress from aspiration to death, from moments that promise glory (even if they are only the infantile fantasies of omnipresence) to the eventual surrender (even if it is only the banal fact of mortality). Tragedy also attunes itself to the sharing of primal guilt, in the practice of ritual and sacrifice, it essentially re-enacts, as well as in durable parables like that of Oedipus. Perhaps great tragedy is that which resists history and retains humanity.

This "scholarly" view of tragedy that evokes some of the most "commonsensical" and time immemorial notions in literature and literary criticism, as we shall try to demonstrate, assumes an ontological basis that holds totalizing notions not only of human suffering but also of the human self. The question of experience and suffering as a human experience is inseparable from the notion of the self in that it is the self that experiences. My attempt in the paper is to show that such a notion of the self as a fixed entity and a theory of literature based on similar assumptions are ideological in content and hence do not hold any universal value. However, the paper is not trying to develop a universal theory of tragedy, but is only making a modest attempt to demonstrate the fact that the so-called self itself was not *it-self* over the ages and hence an essentialist view of tragedy based on such an ontological notion of the self suffers comic limitations. To this end we have chosen Christopher Marlowe's *Doctor Faustus* primarily because it is one of the early Renaissance British plays in which the concept of the self is radically thematized. We propose to seek our difference from more traditional reading of the play in several ways. Whereas a major bulk of Marlowe criticism is engaged in locating the meaning of the play in relation to the actualization of the given potentials of Faustus as man, our main concern in this paper is to explore the potentials of the play as a discursive locus in which multiple notions of the subject emerge and combat. In other words, we are trying to demonstrate the textual constitution of Faustus and further how he moves from one discourse to another, from one particular subject position to its opposite and finally, the relationship between a particular discourse and the kind of subject position(s) it offers. The paper examines how the play registers the different movements of Faustus, how it asks the question as to what Faustus *is* at each point of these movements and finally it throws open the meaning of the play in relation to the meaning of selfhood.

Before we proceed to see how Faustus loses his self (as a result of his pact with devils), we should examine the pre-given self of Faustus, its potentials and limitations—the ways in which the sixteenth century England understood the meaning of the human self. The play presents what the sixteenth century audience could easily understand and identify—the self as a pre-given *thing* labouring under its pre-given predicaments. It should be noted that *Doctor Faustus* is one of the first British plays in which a man "born of parents of base of stock" would become the protagonist. It is also a play in which the protagonist, a common man is presented in nearly complete social isolation. In fact, the only meaningful relationship which he has is with God and His other. Or to reverse the statement, in the context of the play it appears that a relationship can become meaningful or otherwise only if it is a relationship with God. Thus the prologue itself states the theme of the play—man's relationship with God, his possibilities and potentials. The play presents Faustus as the universal man labouring under strict and strictly irreversible universal predicaments. This Renaissance ontology of man elaborated in various writings of the time, we could argue, had a strong epistemological basis in that it was a certain arrangement of knowledge that created this particular notion of the (human) subject. In many subtle ways, *Doctor Faustus* demonstrates the complex relationship between knowledge, power, discourse and the self.

Faustus emerges and grows in the morality where man is only a symbol. Now this newly born child of Renaissance humanism stands on the stage with all his strength and limitations, with the two irrevocable possibilities of salvation and damnation. Above him is the all-powerful heaven and below him, the eternal abyss of perpetual damnation. The 'child' is too weak, too ignorant in terms of choosing what is good for him and so the kind Father sends to the stage the Good Angels and of course, the kind-hearted priests who will guide the child along the path of salvation. It appears from this scheme of things that in the Renaissance perception of the human self, man is essentially given some kind of freedom. It is this kind of a given freedom that characterizes the very being of man. But at the same time it encounters a few paradoxes. On the one hand man is given freedom—the free will to choose and on the other hand he is too ignorant to choose what is good for him and hence the overwhelming need to teach him how to choose. This has the following implications: he should know what he is, what true knowledge is and further how his knowledge can be used to realize his greatest potential and possibility—salvation. In this scheme of things, it appears that the knowledge of the world is inseparable from the knowledge of the self. Further, the knowledge given to the ignorant child of the newly born humanism has to be true knowledge, and true knowledge as authentic knowledge is what appeared in the guise of "the most authentic science"—theology. Thus during the Renaissance, there were universities across Europe where true fruits of theological wisdom and eternal knowledge were imparted to men. Donald Kelley explains this point:

> In Medieval universities master and disciples were subject to its "disciplines" and theology remained "the Queen of Sciences." The universities were fundamentally authoritarian not only in the sense that they privileged certain "authorities," certain traditional authors and indeed defined disciplines in terms of these "auctores" and their "auctoritus." It is true that the standard method of teaching was logical and dialectical, but for the most part of this 'scholastic' method was designed to justify in order to inculcate and to criticize rather than to investigate received doctrines in particular fields of study. . . . In short, this established a framework of Christian knowledge, its expansion, its teaching within which debates

> over human sciences, art and values and goals should be carried on for generations.[4]

Knowledge in the Renaissance Christian framework essentially means knowledge of God and man's place in the world, his possibilities and potentials were defined by this knowledge. Although human existence or rather the meaning of human existence was crucially connected to God, this scheme of thought was liberal enough to grant man a certain amount of freedom and autonomy, celebrated in the Renaissance writing as the 'dignity of man.' To quote another passage from Kelley:

> Renaissance "Anthropology" focused on two basic and interrelated questions, one religious and one philosophical. The first was the problem of free will and the second was the question of knowledge. The second question signified human psychology and the thrust of the 'Renaissance philosophy' of man was directed to the question of knowledge—its possibility, conditions, limits, purpose and values. (48)

Although man is an immediate givenness, this givenness does not give him to know what his givenness is. Therefore he has to deploy his intellectual faculty (a divine gift) in order to seek and realize what his givenness is. This ontological search for the meaning of being, paradoxically, has to be carried out as an ontic search in and through the ontic science of theology. This search, or rather an exercise in understanding and revealing one's self, in the Christian tradition took the form of confession in its different manifestations. One can trace a good example of it in the confessions of St. Augustine. Through his confessions, Augustine reaches not only self-understanding but he also reveals his self-understanding to others. Thus in Augustine self-understanding and self-revelation become inseparable. Both confession and salvation presuppose self-renunciation, but if one has to renounce oneself one should know what one is (renouncing). As a precondition for self-understanding, one has to accept a set of rules, hold certain dogmas as permanent truth, accept authoritarian decisions in matters of truth, not only to believe certain things but also to show that one believes and accepts institutional authority. Foucault demonstrates how most of these ideas find their clearest manifestations in *exomologesis*. To quote a passage from Foucault:

> *Exomologesis* was a ritual of recognizing oneself as a sinner and penitent. It had several characteristics. First you were a penitent for four to ten years, and this status affected your life. There was fasting and there were rules about clothing and prohibition about sex. . . . In the medieval period *exomologesis* became a ritual. . . . Wearing a hair, shirt and ashes, wretchedly dressed, the sinner stands humbled before the church. Then he prostrates himself and kisses the brethren's knee. *Exomologesis* is not a verbal behaviour but the dramatic recognition of one's status as a penitent. It is self-punishment as well as the voluntary expression of the self. . . . Penitence of sin doesn't have as its target the establishing of an identity but serves instead to mark the refusal of the self: the breaking away from the self. Self-revelation is at the same time self-destruction—*exomologesis* is not verbal, it is symbolic, ritual and theatrical.[5]

For an authentic Christian, self as self-knowledge, understood and revealed publicly as self-revelation, gradually leads to self-destruction. This conclusion needs some kind of a clarification. On the one hand one can claim to have a self only if one understands what one is and this self-realization is achieved in the process of self-revelation. But on the other hand confession as a mode of self-realization also is a kind of self-destruction in that in the act of confession one surrenders completely to God and his representatives in this world. Self is understood only at the same time as it is finally given up (to God). In some way, this argument comes frighteningly close to what Heidegger says about the authentic *Dasien*. Heidegger argues that an ordinary *Dasien* lost in the mundane considerations of everyday existence forgets its authentic existential potentials. This leads to an unauthentic existence and from this inauthenticity characterizing his everyday life, *Dasien* is called back to its authentic being. The authentic being of *Dasien*, in Heidegger's view, is being towards death and hence it implies that only when a *Dasien* understands its being towards death, does it become an authentic *Dasien*. This can be explained in the following way: *Dasien* becomes fully authentic only when it understands its absolute possibility, and the absolute possibility of *Dasien* is death i.e., its own impossibility. To translate this idea into more easily understandable terms would mean that man understands his true being only at the point of his death; once again suggesting the close relationship between self-realization and self-destruction.

It is this essential paradox underlying the Christian notion of the self that Faustus encounters at the beginning of the play. Christianity can guarantee you salvation if you are prepared to completely erase your self-identity. Having a self that is not completely surrendered to God is a sin and further such an unwarranted possession runs the risk of being tempted and subsequently losing the self. Drama in England seems to have emerged in the tradition of *exomologesis* where play in the manifold sense of the term is a revelation of the self. A play like *Everyman* stages such a theatrical act of the exposition of the sinner. The moral drawn at the end is clear—you have a self (soul) but you are too immature to keep it, you may be tempted by Satan and his agents, so surrender it or damnation awaits you. *Doctor Faustus* emerges in the same tradition but it breaks with the tradition in many significant ways.

With these general observations on how medieval Europe theoretically understood and practically realized the concept of the self, we shall now turn to *Doctor Faustus*. When the play opens, Faustus is a Christian subject who has gained the kind of knowledge warranted by Christianity. But we also come to understand that he is discontented with the knowledge. He finds theology an insufficient science centred on an essential paradox which demands his death as a precondition for salvation. In the discourse of salvation (Christianity), he finds that he is only a signifier whose signified is elsewhere. He finds that his self is constituted in and defined by the discourse of salvation (Christianity) which is singular and oppressive. His discontentment with Christianity prompts him to separate himself from it and to search for an alternative. At this point black magic seems to be the 'other' of the discourse of salvation and he decides to pursue this alternative knowledge which he hopes would empower him.

Within this circle is Jehovah's name
Forward and backward anagrammatized,
Th'abbreviated names of holy saints,
Figures of every adjunct to the heavens
And characters of signs and erring stars,
By which the spirits are enforced to rise[6] (1.3)

Surprisingly, in his actual practice of black magic, Faustus does not find a counter discourse to the discourse of salvation. In fact, he does not step outside the discourse of salvation but operates within it and after denouncing the signified of the discourse of salvation, he returns to its signifier. This can be substantiated on the basis of the fact that the sign systems he deploys and the incantations he makes are all parts of the discourse of salvation. What Faustus does in actual practice is to re-read or rearrange the discourse of salvation. It is by way of 'anagrammatizing' and 'deconstructing' the discourse of salvation that he evokes the power of the other world. This radical rewriting of the discourse of salvation brings to the surface knowledge and power whose possibilities the discourse of salvation had excluded and kept in the bottomless pit of eternal darkness thus far. This new possibility excites Faustus.

Lines, circles, letters, characters—
Ay, these are those that Faustus most desires.
O, what a world of profit and delight,
Of power, of honour, and omnipotence
Is promised to the studious artisan! (1.1)

Faustus is resolute about his plan to pursue the new art and the word "damnation terrifies him not." He still treats this new knowledge as exterior to himself and to the discourse of salvation and further, he seems to share the belief that man holds knowledge as an object. He writes a bond (text) in his own blood agreeing to separate himself for ever from the possibility of a return to the discourse of salvation and to remain a "spirit in form and substance." It should be noted that at this point Faustus understands his damnation as a certain possibility but a possibility after the (long?) twenty-four years of power and pleasure. Interestingly, his assumptions of heaven and hell, salvation and damnation are still informed by the discourse of salvation. Faustus, it appears, has to further read the text of damnation in order to understand the meaning of damnation in the text of damnation.

Faustus may have reasons to regret that his early plan to wall the city of Wittenburg or to live like an emperor could not be realized. In fact the text of damnation proves that such ambitions are too childish. Faustus asks Mephistopheles to tell him where exactly is the place called hell and the latter answers:

> Hell hath no limits, nor is circumscribed
> In one self place; for where we are is hell,
> And where hell is, there we must ever be. (2.1)

The explanation which fails to satisfy Faustus, can be treated as a definition of hell in the discourse of salvation. The text of damnation unlike the text of salvation does not treat hell as a territory marked out in time and place, but treats it as a question of relation. It seems that in the text of damnation, binary oppositions like hell/heaven, inside/outside, man/woman etc. do not stand as guarantee for truth.

The often-discussed question of the nature of tragic conflict in *Doctor Faustus* can be related to the question of the text of damnation. The tragic conflict in Faustus is the result of his realization that the moment he started reading/writing the text of damnation, he became a part of that. Faustus does not only write a text (bond) of damnation, but he becomes the text that he writes. In other words, Faustus's damnation is a textual act, it is written and signed by him in his own blood (being). Where could Faustus flee after such a pact of sin, what forgivenness after such an act of reading! A divine instruction inscription appears on his body—*Homo, fuge*, but where shall Faustus flee?

The notion of a fixed self that remains unaltered by the text it reads is a fiction that exists only in the discourse of salvation and perhaps also by extension in the Anglo-American literary critical tradition. In the text of damnation as well as in many contemporary schools of criticism, the text and its reader are born at the same time, exactly at the moment when the act of reading begins. If we take the idea of free will seriously, it is true to say that Faustus writes his text of damnation in the sense that Faustus is fully responsible for what happens to him. But it is also true to say that the text of damnation writes Faustus as much as Faustus writes the text of damnation. This idea can be explained in the following way. Once Faustus signs his pact with Satan, once he is outside the discourse of salvation, Faustus is no longer a unified self because the notion of a unified self as a concept is valid only within the discourse of salvation. In other words, once Faustus signs his pact with devils, he cannot be saved and the meaning of his being (self) cannot be traced in relation to the discourse of salvation. In the above quoted lines, Mephistopheles seems to be suggesting that unlike in the humanist tradition, there is no absolute difference between the reader, writer and the text in the text of damnation.

Again, in the text of damnation, time is not an empty something that exists out there without human mediation. Eternity is not something into which one falls one day just by accident, but eternity and time, hell and heaven exist simultaneously in the text of damnation. Damnation is not something that will happen to Faustus after twenty-four years, it has always already happened. Damnation happened to Faustus at the same time as he signed his pact with devils or at the same time as he started reading/writing the text of damnation. In the text of damnation, the long-fallen angels, the Greek beauty and the human Faustus all exist simultaneously. Faustus moves from place to place, back and forth in time and what he finds is unlimited simultaneity. It has no beginning or end, the fragmented text of damnation moves without a telos or subject, it is a continuous flux. That could be the reason why Mephistopheles refuses to answer the question as to who made the world. Are we to understand that according to Mephistopheles the world is not yet made but perhaps is in the process of being made.

Although Faustus has renounced the discourse of salvation, the latter is not prepared to renounce him. The discourse of salvation always presents Faustus with the possibility of a return to the discourse of salvation although (theologically) such a possibility seems too far. Several years after giving up the hope of salvation, and after several years of jubilation without soul, Faustus at times is haunted by a sense of nostalgia. He makes occasional attempts at getting himself reintegrated to the discourse of salvation. He has a nostalgic desire to get integrated into different social institutions. Once again, and perhaps this is what a number of critics seem to be doing, the "tragedy" of Faustus can be seen in the context of this nostalgia. If Faustus can fully overcome his nostalgia, then his experience of the present gets a new meaning and "tragedy" is overcome at the same time as man overcomes his nostalgia for a lost paradise. In his nostalgic desire to get reintegrated to the system he has denounced, Faustus forgets the fact that various relationships including family relations become meaningful only with the discourse of salvation. The text of damnation resists any such nostalgia for self-integration. This is how Mephistopheles replies when Faustus asks for a wife:

> Marriage is a ceremonial toy
> If thou lovest me, think no more of it
> I will cull thee out the fairest courtesans
> And bring them every morning to thy bed. (2.1)

A careful reading of the play would expose the naivete underlying the common assumption that tempted Faustus into damnation. In fact neither Lucifer nor Mephistopheles ever tries to hide from Faustus the atrocities of hell and damnation. The very first appearance of Mephistopheles horrifies Faustus and he asks him to return to him in a less frightening shape. Mephistopheles performs different roles. He is a slave, a master and a friend to Faustus at the same time. In the text of damnation, social hierarchies keep fluctuating and as a result Faustus is a master and a slave and so is Mephistopheles. Interestingly, Mephistopheles remains a friend to Faustus till his last day; he is a lover—"if thou lovest me, think no more of it [marriage]."

Ironically, the temptations come to Faustus from God and his agents. Strictly speaking, for the reader/writer of the text of damnation, salvation is merely a fable. And yet the discourse of salvation presents itself to Faustus an alternative possibility and a vision of what might have been. It is this vision of what might have been (the other possibility for Faustus) that makes Faustus feel guilty at times. The life of Faustus can be said to be tragic only if one sees his damnation against the possibility of what it might have otherwise been. This is exactly what the Good Angel and other agents of God do in the play—stop Faustus from enjoying his newly-won freedom, his jubilation without soul. Once Faustus has signed his pact with Lucifer, it is doubtful if he can be saved at all, and the Good Angel and the Old Man know this fact. And yet they keep haunting him with a vision of what he has lost forever, making him feel guilty and miserable. They present him with a vision of Christ's blood in the sky where it is too far and too late for Faustus to reach. The question that the discourse of salvation has to answer is—why trying to pretend to save Faustus when he cannot be saved at all? Lucifer says:

> Christ cannot save thy soul for he is just
> There is none but I have interest in the same. (2.3)

How are we to take these words of the arch devil? Lucifer seems to have been always truthful to Faustus. He never gave any false promise to Faustus nor did he hide the atrocities of damnation from him. It appears from all these facts that it is the discourse of salvation that tries to torment its opponent with various versions of what looks like a lost opportunity for Faustus.

At this stage, one might also be prompted to ask the meaning of the term damnation. In the text of damnation, Mephistopheles keeps permanently fluctuating and might even argue that there is no more a damnation for Faustus because he is already damned in the sense that he is already the text of damnation, he is the text that he wrote. Then Faustus's damnation becomes possible and possibly meaningful only within the discourse of salvation. In other words, what happens to Faustus after twenty-four years of his signing the pact with devils can become meaningful or meaningless only with reference to the discourse of salvation. The disturbing and final question is—what meaning in hell? Hell as a concept is a creation of the discourse of salvation and as such it is meaningful within that particular discourse, but what meaning in hell? The discourse of salvation defines hell as meaninglessness; it marks the limit of meaning. If hell is the end of meaning, what meaning in hell? Faustus who began by asking the meaning of hell now finds himself in the hell of meaning and now where shall Faustus flee?

Certainly Faustus does not use his power to accomplish some of his early plans, but this cannot be treated as a tragic failure in Faustus. One might argue that with the help of devils and at the cost of his soul Faustus could perform nothing more than a few silly games. But what such arguments fail to realize is the basic nature of the reading of the text of damnation. To be in the text of damnation, to be reading the text of damnation is to remain caught in an endless game in which meanings are always provisional and they are not related to any single transcendental signified. To read the text of damnation (as Faustus does) is to enter into an endless game in which along with the games one plays he makes and remakes oneself. Here the self is not a given fixed entity, but something which one makes and remakes for oneself according to one's convenience. Faustus's last long speech in the play, strictly speaking, is not a monologue: there are so many voices in the voice of Faustus. Faustus is no longer a single united self—he is irreducibly and irrevocably plural now. At this stage of realizing himself as different from himself, once again he thinks of the self (soul), but this time he speaks as if every part of his body contained his soul.

> You stars that reigned my nativity
> Whose influence hath allotted death and hell
> Now draw up Faustus, like a foggy mist
> Into the entrails of your labouring clouds
> That when you vomit forth into the air
> My limbs may issue from your smoky mouths,
> So that my soul may but ascend to heaven (5.2)

One has reasons to wonder whether Faustus is making parody of the concepts of heaven and hell in these lines. Faustus who feels the pain of fragmentation knows that one of the ways of countering fragmentation is by opting for more fragmentation. He curses his origin and movement, the books he read in his youth and wishes to be an animal as an animal does not have to worry about the soul. As Faustus moves from text to text, he loses his pre-constituted self (granted to him by Christianity) and becomes a plural self. Finally, damnation could happen to Faustus because he retains his self that could create and recreate it in different ways. As against this, the old man in the play cannot be damned because he has surrendered himself to the discourse of salvation. The moral question ultimately is whether to have a self and lose it or not to have a self and never lose it. One may not call it a heroic deed, but Faustus opts for the first and this is his "tragedy." The Renaissance reader tries to read the meaning of the self, not in the discourse of salvation, but in the texts that Christianity prohibited during the medieval ages. Through the various magical feats that he performs, through the games he plays, Faustus understands his difference from others, his difference from the discourse of salvation and finally, his difference from *himself*. This ultimately irreducible, pure difference is death. The fate of Faustus is sealed and will never be altered—he is irreversibly pluralized and he has to move endlessly in and through the text of damnation because the text of damnation unlike the discourse of salvation moves without any teleology, such a text has no end.

NOTES

1. Michel Foucault, *The Use of Pleasure: The History of Sexuality*, trans. Robert Hurley (London: Penguin Books, 1992), Vol. 2, p. 9.
2. Bertolt Brecht, *The Messingkauf Dialogues*, trans. John Willett (London: Methuen, 1965), p. 48.
3. Robert N. Watson, "Tragedy," *The Cambridge Companion to English Renaissance Drama*, ed. A.R. Braunmuller and Michael Hattay (New York: Cambridge Univ. Press, 1990), p. 301.
4. Donald R. Kelly, *Renaissance Humanism* (Boston: Twayne, 1991), p. 35.
5. Michel Foucault, *The Care of the Self*, trans. Robert Hurley (New York: Pantheon, 1986), p. 84.
6. Christopher Marlowe, *Doctor Faustus*, David Bevington and Eric Rasmussen (Oxford: Oxford Univ. Press, 1995).

Darkness in Shakespearean Tragedy with Special Reference to *Macbeth*

CASHMERE MAINDARKAR

Early English drama consisted of mystery and miracle plays dealing with events in the Bible. By 1400 A.D. morality plays were staged featuring characters who represented good or evil. Tragedy made its debut in England after the Renaissance. Its effect was "the arousal of pity and fear."

Put simply, a tragedy is a serious drama that ends in disaster. William Shakespeare was the principal tragic dramatist of the Elizabethan period. His tragedies are noted for their suspense-filled plots, insights into human nature and powerful poetic dialogue.

The gap between the learned and popular audiences had been bridged by playwrights like Thomas Kyd (*The Spanish Tragedy*), Christopher Marlowe, John Lyly, George Peele and Robert Greene (*Friar Bacon and Friar Bungay*). Shakespeare built on the foundation they had laid. He borrowed from fiction, history, myths and earlier plays. But he perfected the dramatic techniques of earlier playwrights. His dramatic poetry is unequalled and he had a genius for probing character, producing emotion and relating human experience to broad philosophical issues. He himself was educated in the two greatest seats of learning: the Theatre and the World. "All the World's stage, and all the men and women merely players. They have their exits and entrances. And one man in his time, plays many parts." His power of poetic expression and character-creation turned his writings into something lively and beautiful. Elizabethan drama was noted for its passion and vitality. Robert Bridges observes: "The interest in a Shakespearean Tragedy lies chiefly in the hero's conduct and is greater as his conduct surprises while it satisfies: and from the constitution of things it is difficult to imagine a character or personality whose actions shall be at once consistent and surprising." Yet Shakespeare's blend of consistency and surprise are immensely believable. Let us consider his four greatest tragedies, *Othello, King Lear, Hamlet* and *Macbeth*, in the light of these statements.

Othello, the Moor of Venice is written in a magnificent operative style. The characters are very human and are full of the faults and follies of men. Iago's scheming, Othello's jealousy, Desdemona's loyalty, Emilia's hysterics—they are all very believable human traits. The darkness in this tragedy is the trouble caused by Othello's jealousy. The darkness is symbolically present in the drama as the evil that lurks in men's hearts to pull down all that is above itself but not quite beyond.

King Lear is a family melodrama. The symbolic darkness here is two-fold: (1) In the King's mind and his ignorance of his daughters' actual intentions. (2) In the hearts of his two elder daughters. Cordelia's character has no evil in her and so her death is more poignant.

In *Hamlet, Prince of Denmark*, Shakespeare dramatizes an old, well-known story and assumes that his audience would fill up the gaps. The verse is meditative. Put briefly, the story explores a sensitive and cultured man's revolt from the carnality and grossness of human life. Darkness comes to the stage as the very First Act takes place at night. Among the shadows of the Castle Platform, the ghost of Hamlet's father arises to present the supernatural element. The new king's dark deeds and punishable offences present evil in black light, as does the Queen's inexplicable behaviour.

According to Quiller-Couch, "*Macbeth* bears a resemblance unique among Shakespeare's writings to Greek tragedy." While Hamlet expatiates melodiously upon what he cannot begin to do, Macbeth expatiates even more melodiously upon what he cannot cease from doing. Coleridge comments: "Of all Shakespeare's plays *Macbeth* is the most rapid, *Hamlet* the slowest in movement."

Darkness in *Macbeth* is not limited to the symbolical level as in *King Lear* and *Othello*, but also reaches the physical level—the stage (as in *Hamlet*). Shakespeare's handling of the supernatural agencies, the three witches, is a great triumph. The three sisters lay the foundation of the main plot and have been referred to as the 'instruments of darkness.' Macbeth is a good man who fights valiantly for his King, but he is also an ambitious man. His inner conflict between his scruples and his evil ambition is resolved by Lady Macbeth who removes his inhibitions and inflames his ambition.

Lady Macbeth is peerless alike in triumph and defeat. She is the one who kills her husband's conscience but ends up with a troubled one, herself. Her grief is not shared. Her anxiety can end only in death, for her soul is besieged by the burden of her crimes. The image of the bloody dagger, the hands she must wash clean, "But damned spot, out I say," beautifully portray her anguish. Shakespeare has depicted ambition as a vice and as in all his plays vice is vicious and forgiveness is the supreme virtue. Unlike Ben Jonson who wrote corrective comedies, Shakespeare never undertook the responsibility of reforming society. He merely entertained and the people perceived the morals for themselves.

Even in *Macbeth*, he leads us through a series of events representing the dark longings of an evil heart. "My thought, whose murder yet is but fantastical," receives the boost from the instruments of darkness, that

> look like the innocent flower,
> but he the serpent under it.
> the deed, MURDER in all its hideousness
> I go and it is done. The bell invites me; Hear it not, Duncan,
> for it is a knell that summons thee to heaven or to hell.

The success of evil gaining power, "Fair is foul and foul is fair" but losing sleep, 'Methought I heard a voice cry,' "Sleep no, more Macbeth does murder sleep, the innocent sleep"—and the final victory of good over evil. In fact the darkness in all Shakespearean tragedies represents evil in various forms. An evil which seems all-encompassing and overpowering at first, is defeated by the agents of morality, ending in the victory of good over it.

Songs in Shakespeare's *King Lear*

MADHURI S. GOKHALE

In *The Merchant of Venice*, Lorenzo says to Jessica,

> The man that hath no music in himself,
> Nor is moved with concord of sweet sounds,
> Is fit for treasons, stratagems and spoils,
> The motions of his spirit are dull as night,
> And his affections dark as Erebus
> Let no such man be trusted.

These lines highlight the significance of music, and also express Shakespeare's devotion to music. The Elizabethan notion was that the created universe was itself in a state of music, and that it was one perpetual dance. The Elizabethan age is often referred to as the golden age of the English song. The song was an integral and essential part of the dramatic structure.

Songs have been a common feature on the stage. Song, dance and drama evolved together in a ritual dance. Shakespeare was not the only one, nor even the first one to use songs in tragedies. Thomas Kyd in *The Spanish Tragedy* and Thomas Sackville in *Gorboduc* have used songs in tragedies. Aristotle regarded the song as one of the essential elements of every tragedy.

Music was a significant part of Shakespeare's workshop, next to the arts of poetry and drama. The impact of any of his plays would not suffer greatly if gunshot and processions, fencing and costumes were eliminated, but the actual sound of vocal and instrumental music is essential to Shakespeare's purpose. The traditional associations of music often play their part in providing the play with a network of wider associations. The evocative and symbolic functions of music are integral elements of what has been called the world-picture of Elizabethans. The great peculiarity of music as an art is that the sounds which comprise its medium can be produced in two ways—by playing on specially constructed instruments and by using vocal cords in a special way. We find a variety of songs in Shakespeare's plays, namely plain songs, catches, descants, airs and madrigals. Out of the thirty-seven plays of Shakespeare, thirty-two contain interesting references to music and there are around a hundred songs in the plays.

According to W.H. Auden, there are two kinds of songs in Shakespeare's plays, the called-for and the impromptu, and they serve different dramatic purposes. A called-for song is a song which is sung by one character, at the request of another who wishes to hear music. Consequently there are very few called-for songs in the tragedies, where the steady advance of the hero towards his doom must not be interrupted. The impromptu singer breaks into a song to relieve his feelings in a way that speech cannot do. The uncalled-for music indeed has a tremendous impact in tragedies where songs come out spontaneously. The revelations made by an impromptu song are comic or pathetic rather than shocking.

Most of Shakespeare's plays are characterized by the intermixing of two genres—tragedy and comedy. The practice of mixing the tragic and the comic elements goes against the classical norms. Philip Sidney in 'An Apology for Poetry' says, "It is foolish to mingle kings and clowns or to match hornpipes and funerals." While watching the performance of *King Lear*, we may ask the question, "Is the Fool's presence consonant with the high, serious tone of tragedy?" Certainly yes, as Shakespeare represents the life in its true spirit by mixing the tragic and the comic. The cathartic role of songs intensifies the mood of the tragedy. Thus, Shakespeare's plays are not in the rigid sense either tragedies or comedies, but as Johnson says, 'they are compositions of a distinct kind, exhibiting the real state of sublunary nature.' In Shakespeare's plays the songs were directed towards the delineation of character, the clarification of the setting, the promotion of action, and pure entertainment. This paper aims at examining the function of songs in *King Lear* as they appear in the Quarto edition, and to focus on the following factors:

(i) This is o.k. Why do only two particular characters in this tragedy sing songs?
(ii) Why is a particular piece of music placed just where it is and not somewhere else?
(iii) Why are the words of the songs what they are?
(iv) What effect do the songs have upon the spectators?

Because of the nature of Lear's internal conflict, his stubborn resistance to the humbling forces unleashed against him, the devices of self-revelation so commonly used by Elizabethan dramatists—soliloquies, asides and conversations with a confidant—are not open to Shakespeare in this play. Lear cannot debate within himself, nor surrender his pride so far as to confide in anyone. The condition of his ordeal is that he fails to recognize his own weaknesses and dependence on others. Naturally he cannot admit the self-doubt and soul-searching regret, which Hamlet and Macbeth give voice to. Shakespeare was therefore faced with the technical problem of how to present to the audience Lear's guilt and folly, and in answer he produced the Fool. The Fool with the aid of brilliant snatches carries out this job effectively. The function that the chorus had in Greek tragedy is carried out here by the Fool who is licensed "To speak what he feels." His songs represent the fragmentation of the world. They share the quality of expressing through simple juxtaposition of images what more logically structured dramatic dialogue cannot express.

Shakespeare carefully considered the talents of his actors. In his writing of plays, there is a marked difference after 1598, when Robert Armin succeeded Will Kempe. Armin was an actor, capable of greater subtlety, better able to communicate the complexity and depth of characterization and also an accomplished singer. It is said that the roles of Touchstone in *As You Like It*, Feste in *Twelfth Night* and the Fool in *King Lear* were specifically created to take advantage of his outstanding singing ability.

Most of Shakespeare's songs are not original. However, the fact that he borrowed from others does not matter much. Shakespeare perfected what he found and through his imagination, poetic gifts and broad outlook made a remarkable use of these songs, thereby heightening the tragedy.

It is interesting to note that the first three songs of the Fool which occur in I.iv are both semantically and logically related to each other, in certain ways. His first song 'That lord that counsell'd thee' in an ironic way establishes Lear as 'a bitter fool.' His second song serves both to characterize him as a 'natural' and to illuminate the relationship in which he stands to Lear. The lines,

> Fools had ne'er less grace in a year,
> For wise men are grown foppish;
> And know not how their wits to wear,
> Their manners are so apish.

depict that the Fool is the self-deposed King's better reason, and his impudent and riddling wit is meant to make Lear aware of his own folly. The last two lines of this song are ambiguous. They may mean either that wise men in imitating fools are at a loss to manage the wit they should be using, or that fools are getting so much competition from wise men that the fools do not know what face to put on their own natural wittiness. Malone points out that in this song Shakespeare was echoing some popular song or rhyme of the day. That Lear pays full attention to the comments made by the Fool is evident from the question which immediately precedes this song. Lear says to the Fool, "When were you wont to be so full of songs, Sirrah?"

The next song 'then they for sudden joy did weep' is related to the second song. Where the earlier song had included the King in the roster of fools through the syllogism that he is a man, and all men are fools from birth, this song more audaciously calls Lear by a title which he has earned for himself. It seems likely that the song is a parody of the opening lines of a famous ballad of those times. Thus, the three songs have a semantic connection as well as internal logical relations. It can be clearly seen that when the songs have a very close relationship among themselves, there is very little intervening prose between them.

The word 'Fool' runs through a spectrum of meanings throughout the play. In successive speeches, Lear calls the world 'a great stage of fools' and himself 'The natural fool of fortune.' The Fool encompasses this range of meanings in a song "That sir which serves and seeks for gain." It provides a microscopic statement of the whole idea of *King Lear*. Through this song, the Fool gives Lear moral guidance. The song is sung at a point when both Goneril and Regan have turned away from Lear. The song offers deep insights into psychological truths. Thus, as in most Hindi movies, Shakespeare does not use a song "for its own sake"; rather, it has a vital function in the framework of the play. The aim of the songs is to enable the audience to assimilate the deeper sense of the tragedy.

When Lear is at the height of terror and the tempest, the Fool sings,

> He that hath a little tiny wit,
> With hey, ho, the wind and the rain,
> Must make content with his fortunes fit,
> For the rain it raineth everyday.

Shakespeare has taken these lines from his earlier play *Twelfth Night*, and has made some minor changes. At this point in the play, both Lear and Fool are out in the wind and the rain, and have by necessity to content themselves with the fortunes which have befallen them. The song is perfectly congruent with the surrounding text. The moral of the Fool's song is that men must sometimes be content merely to endure the circumstances in which they find themselves. Lear, who can respond to this moral of the song by asserting 'true, my boy,' is a Lear who fifty lines later in the play will be concerned about "the houseless poverty of those naked children."

Lear's suffering is not merely psychological, but also physical. The King probably gets wet for the first time in his life; and it is extremely difficult for Lear to endure this suffering. All the songs give a kind of phonic pleasure to the spectators, and help substantially in making Lear's lot endurable to them. In Act 4, scene 7, when Cordelia agrees to have her father awakened, the Doctor says, "Louder the Music There." Here music is used not only as a part of atmosphere, but also as a therapy. The soft music restores "the untuned and jarring senses of the King."

In a play, songs are more apt to indicate to an audience changes of tone within the play. In I.iv when Lear is angry over Goneril's disposition, the Fool tries to divert Lear's anger by singing the refrain of an old song "whoop jug! I love thee!"

The Fool's last song 'come o'er the bourn, Bessy, to me' seems to be an oblique comment on the all-powerful emotion of love. Once King Lear has gone through the school of the Clown's philosophy, the Fool disappears by the end of Act 3. But even after the Fool disappears, Edgar's songs in the form of mad utterances play a very crucial role. Songs like Tom O'Bedlam which were called 'mad-songs' were very commonly sung in England in the seventeenth century. The act of singing gives Edgar a kind of relief as he can allow his bitter fury to be released. Through songs, he begs for love that had been denied to him. Edgar's songs are grotesque, ugly and full of repulsive imagery. They highlight the point that evil is omnipresent in life; and even a virtuous person cannot escape it. They are a critique of the whole situation. It takes the commentary on the evil a little further. In his song,

> Horse to ride, and weapons to wear,
> But mice and rats and such small deer
> Have been Tom's food for seven long years.

Tom seems a paradigm of mere appetite ingesting the scum of nature. This relentless emphasis on the physical body—what it eats, how it is punished, what it wears—marks Tom's complete fall to the bottom of the lake of darkness. It makes Lear's belief "our basest beggars are in the poorest thing superfluous" seem optimistic by comparison.

Edgar's songs have a kind of dual role to play. They not only emphasize his pathetic condition, but also constantly remind us of Lear's tragic state. Thus the songs in the sub-plot are related to the main plot.

In his song 'Be thy mouth or black or white,' the disorder of the dogs getting out of the hatch and Edgar's promise to "throw" his head, allude clearly to the Aesopic story of the Hart, which being too much in love with his head had lost his reason and was destroyed by the hound. Here the reference is also to Lear who did lose his head in self-love.

Edgar's chant "child Rowland to the dark Tower came" inspired Browning to write one of his most remarkable poems, which has the same title. Edgar's song 'sleepest or wakest thou jolly shepherd' emphasizes the necessity of the ruler to be for ever watchful in the interest of justice.

Thus, the uses of vocal songs in Shakespeare's plays were manifold, and always purposeful, ranging from appropriate moments of pure entertainment to complete and indispensable integration with the play, in order to illuminate the character and carry the action forward. The concrete manner in which the vocal and instrumental effects are integrated into the total structure of the play is highly remarkable. Songs give a very fine texture to his plays and enrich its quality. It has been said that Shakespeare's works have inspired more music than have the combined works of all other notable poets. While statistical demonstration of this assertion has never been attempted, it may nevertheless be regarded as substantially true. His effective use of songs reveals his supreme craftsmanship. We must not regard Shakespeare's songs as a divertissement for which other pieces might easily be substituted. Their effect is carefully calculated in dramatic and poetic terms, and therefore they are functional, rather than decorative.

Imagery in Shakespeare's *Macbeth*: A Study

N.M. ASTON

In *Macbeth*,[1] William Shakespeare makes use of the simplest and humblest of things of everyday life. The good and evil qualities of human beings are revealed through them. *Macbeth* as a play is both metaphysical and worldly in nature. The imagery in *Macbeth* is more rich and varied, more imaginative than in any other play.

Shakespeare introduces us to three witches who predict a glorious future for Macbeth. The third witch says.

> All hail, Macbeth! that shalt be King hereafter! (I.iii.51)

By the use of images, Shakespeare has made that which is beyond the physical, physical. The whole supernatural order is brought home by the use of appealing images.

When Macbeth takes up new positions, he seems to be a round peg in a square hole. The position does not seem to fit him. Macbeth seems to be wearing garments belonging to someone else. This has, in fact, struck Macbeth in the beginning. After hearing the prophecies of the witches, Macbeth wonders how they would come true. In the meantime Rosse comes from the king and greets him as Thane of Cawdor, to which Macbeth answers, rather shockingly:

> The Thane of Cawdor lives: why do you dress me
> In borrowed robes? (I.iii.109)

Macbeth sees that the prophecy has, in reality, come true. He begins to think of the other prophecies when Banquo says,

> New honours come upon him,
> Like our strange garments, cleave not to their mould
> But with the aid of us. (I.iii.147-48)

Thus the metaphor of clothes is used twice. The garments are too loose on Macbeth. The image goes on to show that Macbeth is not fit for his new position.

Pleased with Macbeth, King Duncan decides to pay a visit to his castle. Macbeth feels it to be a fine situation to bring the other prophecy true, (of course) by killing Duncan. However, he hesitates in the deed as he knows that he is the host and that the King has always been kind to him. Macbeth explains to his wife that he feels immensely guilty in doing the deed and that he would not like to upset the smooth situation. He uses the metaphor of clothes again:

> I have bought
> Golden opinions from all sort of people,
> Which would be worn now in their newest gloss,
> Not cast aside so soon. (I.vii.31-34)

Hearing this abrupt and unexpected change in Macbeth, his wife replies:

> Was the hope drunk
> Wherein you dress'd yourself? (I.vii.35-36)

At last owing to the continuous chase by Lady Macbeth, Macbeth commits the treacherous murder of Duncan. Macbeth, the Thane of Cawdor, is to become the King of Scotland. Rosse tells Macduff that he is going to 'scone' for the coronation of Macbeth. After hearing this, Macduff employs the metaphor of clothes:

> Well, may you see things well done there! Adieu,
> Lest our old robes sit easier than our new. (II.iv.37-38)

Later, in Act V, Menteth announces that the English power is near, led by Macbeth, his uncle Siward and Macduff. Cathness sees Macbeth as a man vainly fastening a large garment on him with a very small belt; but, for certain,

> He cannot buckle, his distemper's cause
> Within the belt of rule. (V.ii.15-16)

In reply, he again says:

> Now does he feel his title
> Hang loose about him, like a giant's robe
> Upon a dwarfish thief. (V.iii.20-22)

Macbeth, repenting on having killed Duncan, speaks in images, using Cherubim, the angel of the highest order, naked like a new-born babe, striding the blast and pleading:

> Or heaven's cherubim hors'd
> Upon the sightless couriers of the air,
> Shall blow the horrid deed in every eye,
> That tears shall drown the wind. (I.vii.22-25)

The whole picture echoes in sound again. The same image strikes us when Rosse goes to tell Macduff that Macbeth has killed his wife and children. Rosse says:

> But I have words
> That would be howl'd out in the desert air
> Where hearing should not latch them. (IV.iii.192-94)

We are again given to think that light stands for good deeds, as when Duncan tells Malcolm:

> But sign of nobleness, live stars, shall shine
> On all deserters. (I.iv.41-42)

That darkness stands for bad deeds is clear from the soliloquy of Macbeth:

Stars, hide your fires;
Let not light see my black and deep desire.
The eye wink at the hand; yet let that be
Which the eye fears, when it is done, to see. (I.iv.50-55)

However, Lady Macbeth thinks nothing much of them; she compares such deeds to pictures painted on a wall:

It is the eye of childhood that fear painted devil.

Macbeth feels that sin is a disease. He asks the doctor to cure Scotland of its disease.

And purge it to a sound and pristine health
I would applaud thee to the very echo.
That should applaud again. Pull't off, I say.
Would scour these English hence? (V.iv.53-57)

It must be noted that Macbeth's images are soothing and through them we feel his longing for peace of mind. His greatest trouble is that he has murdered sleep. The constant images of blood increase the feeling of fear, horror, pain and disgust as in Macbeth's description of himself wading in a river of blood. However, the outstanding image among these is the speech of Lady Macbeth when she says:

Here's the smell of the blood still
All the perfumes of Arabia will not sweeten this little hand. (V.i.46-47)

Besides, there are many animal images throughout the play—venomous serpent, chickens, bear, tiger, rhinoceros and so on.

The play reveals that it is better that people assess their aptitude and weigh the pros and cons of their real ability, before embarking on any work. However human nature is not so submissive as one would think and we could only satisfy them by employing another image:

Hover through the fog and fitting air.
Fair is foul, and foul is fair.

NOTE

1. William Shakespeare, *Macbeth*, ed. Andrew M. Wilkinson (London: University Tutorial Press, 1966).

Love, Marriage and the Status of Women in Shakespeare's *The Taming of the Shrew*

PRABHA SAMPATH

It is March 8th today—a day observed the world over as Women's Day and I'm delighted to present a paper that deals with two areas that have always evoked my passionate interest and deep commitment—Shakespeare and women's studies. With that preliminary observation, I shall stick my neck out and court controversy right away by reading out those infamous speeches by Petruchio and Kate respectively that have made this play so problematic.

> I will be master of what is mine own.
> She is my goods, my chattels, she is my house,
> My household stuff, my field, my barn,
> My horse, my ox, my ass, my any thing . . . (III.ii)
> Thy husband is thy lord, thy life, thy keeper,
> Thy head, thy sovereign . . .
> Such duty as the subject owes the prince,
> Even such, a woman oweth to her husband;
> And when she is froward, peevish, sullen, sour,
> And not obedient to his honest will,
> What is she but a foul contending rebel
> And graceless traitor to her loving lord?
> I am ashamed that women are so simple
> To offer war where they should kneel for peace;
> Or seek for rule, supremacy, and sway
> When they are bound to serve, love, and obey. (V.ii)

If you're at a loss for words to express your anger and revulsion, the best brains in the business can help you. Bernard Shaw found the play "altogether disgusting to modern sensibility"; Sir Quiller-Couch thought "the whole Petruchio business tiresome and offensive." In a book called *Bad Shakespeare* published in the 1980s, a feminist scholar called Shirley Garner suggests that we stop prescribing, teaching or discussing the play with our students.

My concern is not with these critics. My concern is with students who are disturbed by the ideas, put off by the language and horrified by the whole picture of the man-woman relationship that seems to be unfolding. What was William Shakespeare then? Some kind of a racist, sexist, Fascist, anti-semitic—vide Othello, Kate, Coriolanus and Shylock? Among other things I consider it my peculiar misfortune to hear umpteen people—students in debates, men in arguments and anti-Shakespeareans out to make a point—umpteen thousand people quote the Prince of Denmark out of context: "Frailty, thy name is woman!" Shakespeare was an M.C.P.—Q.E.D.

The purpose I fondly hope to serve by this paper is to check this kind of rash and hasty generalization on the part of students. "To generalize is to be a fool" said Blake—and generalizations of this kind are especially dangerous with Shakespeare. He is not the kind of writer one sums up on the basis of single lines (or whole speeches) quoted out of context. I'm not trying to sell you the notion of the elusive profound genius whose philosophy of life you can't attempt to write a precis on. I'm only trying to tell you that he is par excellence the chameleon dramatist who does not wear his heart on his sleeve.

The point at issue is this: Does the play degrade the role of women in society—the wife in marriage? Is the story of the taming of Kate an obnoxious, primitive farce which the patriarchal society of the Elizabethans found hilarious and appealing? Are the views expressed in Kate's final speech indicative of the abject surrender and total submission of the spirited heroine? How does the play view man-woman relationships? And the question that none of us can answer: are the views expressed here Shakespeare's own? I would like to examine these issues in the old fashioned way of my undergraduate days—by a close look at the text, to see what answers we can find there to such questions.

Love, as the poet said, is certainly a many splendour'd thing—but it is safe to say that perhaps no other writer saw its heights and depths, its glories and griefs, its triumphs and its tragedies and equally its absurdities, follies and inconsistencies as Shakespeare did. It is this totality of vision which make his comedies of love so intelligent, so down-to-earth, no matter if they are set in Padua, Illyria, Arden or Athens. In the landmark work that drew the attention of the twentieth century readers to Shakespeare's comedies, H.B.Charlton was the first to point out that Shakespeare walks the tight rope between comedy and romance with such finesse that he avoids the extreme pitfalls of excessive sentiment and mindless farce. Charlton of course did not think much of *The Shrew*—according to him it was a farce which went wrong—an experiment that Shakespeare was never to repeat again.

The later twentieth century has learnt to look at the early comedies less patronizingly, more appreciatively. For instance, it is now considered utterly simplistic to regard the Bianca-Lucentio plot as "romantic" and the Petruchio-Katherine story as "realistic" or "farcical." Shakespeare's art shows scant respect for such boundaries and his genius lay in transcending them. We only have to look below the surface to realize that the so-called romance is only a veneer behind which we find hard-headed realism; and behind the facade of the slap-stick and farce, there is a delightful element of romance. Consider, for example, the opening of the main play. Lucentio has arrived in "Fair Padua, nursery of arts" to "institute a course of learning and ingenious studies"; but a chance encounter with Baptisa's fair daughter—and the books are forgotten. Well might Tranio ask:

> I pray sir, tell me, is it possible
> That love should of a sudden take such hold?

And the answer is yes! It is the virtually incurable love-at-first-sight with its severest symptoms. As the Arden editor Brian Morris points out, "nothing could be more blatantly Petrarchan" than the smitten lover's sighs:

Tranio, I burn, I pine, I perish Tranio
If I achieve not this young modest girl.

It is often regretted that as Indian students of Shakespeare, we are denied access to stage performances of the plays; but look at the benefit reading and rereading the plays with hindsight can confer on us. In Bianca's silence the young lover perceives "maid's mild behaviour and sobriety"; "sacred and sweet" is all that he sees in her, as opposed to Kate's "curst, shrewd" ways. To appreciate the delicious irony of these remarks in the full light of Bianca's scheming, manipulative ways is to discover the underlying themes of Appearance and Reality, Seeming and Being, the ideals of Self-knowledge and Metamorphosis that characterize Shakespearean comedy. It is not just that the scales will fall off our eyes (and ears) when we get to know Bianca better; but the romantic lover Lucentio turns out to be so dull-witted that clever servants have to write, direct, produce, act and stage-manage his love-affair to its eventual success. Here we have a romantic sub-plot (if you still want to call it that) which will end with the mild, modest, sacred and sweet Bianca snapping at her loving husband for whom she has lost 100 crowns with her intransigence: "The more fool you, for laying on my duty." Who are we to disagree with a woman's superior knowledge and accurate judgement of the man she married?

If we take the Petruchio-Katherine main plot, it has inauspicious beginnings indeed, with knockabout farce—literally knockabout—what with the knocking at Hortensio's door and the "knocking" bestowed on Grumio by his master; and here is Petruchio's barefaced avowal:

I come to wive it wealthily in Padua
If wealthily, then happily in Padua.

Hardly an auspicious beginning for a love story! To quote the knocked-about Grumio

Why, nothing comes amiss, so money comes withal.

This brings us to yet another major issue raised in the play—the economics of marriage in Padua. The bargaining is brisk indeed:

> Signor Baptisa, my business asketh haste,
> And everyday I cannot come to woo . . .
> Tell me, if I get your daughter's love
> What dowry shall I have with her to wife?

A mention of the dreadful word "dowry" for us in India is like the proverbial red rag to a bull. But let us take note of the fact that the shrewish Kate does not need to be palmed off with a greater portion than her mild, virtuous, soft-spoken sister. Baptisa is categorical:

> After my death, the one half of my lands
> And in possession twenty thousand crowns.

All this does not come on a platter; for dowry is a two-edged weapon in Padua; in his turn, Petruchio avows:

> And for that dowry I'll assure her of
> Her widowhood, be it that she survive me,
> In all my lands and leases whatsoever.

And this is no empty promise either:

> Let specialties be drawn between us,
> That covenants may be kept on either hand.

The truth is, as Shakespeare knew to his cost, covenants were not often kept up. One of the few precious surviving documents[1] about Shakespeare tells us of his involvement as a witness in such a dowry case—the now famous Belott-Mountjoy case—a suit launched by a son-in-law against his father-in-law in 1612, the documents of which were not brought to light until the present century. Mountjoy, the girl's father and Shakespeare's landlord, promised his son-in-law a portion of 60 pounds, and after his death an inheritance of 200 pounds for his daughter. Instead, all that he gave them was the paltry sum of 10 pounds and some household stuff. Eventually the irate son-in-law and daughter took Mountjoy to court and no less a person than William Shakespeare was summoned to testify. He did depose in the preliminary hearings—only to recall that a dowry had been promised, but he could not remember how much. He did not testify again, and we do not know how that intriguing story ended—whether the sum of money was ever paid.

We must not for a moment imagine that Petruchio is the sole offender as a mercenary lover in Shakespeare's plays. Bassanio, in the *Merchant of Venice*, is a blatant fortune-hunter, and has nothing to offer his heiress wife except his good looks and dissolute ways. When King Lear cuts off Cordelia without a penny, an aspiring suitor, the Duke of Burgundy, refuses to touch her with a barge pole; but then again, a dowerless orphan, Helena in *All's Well* obtains the hand of the wealthy young Bertram through the intercession of the king; the Countess Olivia falls in love with a penniless page boy; and princess Imogen secretly marries the poor but worthy Posthumus Leonatus, an orphan who has lived in her father's court since childhood.

The point of this is that marriage definitely had its economic and financial implications for the Elizabethans as for Shakespeare. But the gusto and openness with which the business of dowry is discussed in our play has one more side to it; it assured the woman of her right to her father's property and her economic independence in the event of her widowhood. A.L. Rowse, the Elizabethan historian, points out that even without the kind of generous settlement that Petruchio is willing to make, widows had by right one-third of their husband's estate, giving them a great advantage in the marriage market. The Duchess of Lennox and the Duchess of Deveraux were each married four times, each time improving their social status and financial position. So great was the financial attraction of marrying a widow (so Rowse informs us) that Parliament even contemplated a Bill to discourage the practice on demographic counts.

If Petruchio bargains to marry Kate, then Bianca's match can only be described as an auction; here the tables are turned: the father of the girl makes no promises, only demands:

> . . . He of both
> That can assure my daughter the greatest dower
> Shall have my Bianca's love.

Talk about the price one pays for love! And so Bianca is sold to the highest bidder—but we will do well to remember amidst the catalogues of plate and gold, Tyrian tapestry, ivory coffers, cypress chests, apparel, tents and canopies and the like—Tranio has *no claim whatsoever to the wealth he bids*. He is a poseur, a proxy wooer, disguised as Lucentio, son of the rich Vincentio. And if there is a suggestion that Marriage is a Sale or Purchase agreement made between men who have unchallenged political, economic and social power over women—then we will also do well to remember that Baptisa is outwitted and overwhelmed psychologically by his daughter—though his worldly power is never in doubt.

In an age which uses women to sell everything from automobiles to whiskey and cigarettes, in an age which has only just half-heartedly legislated to ensure the property rights of daughters, in an age when women in West and East still have to go to court to claim maintenance rights—it amazes me that we should have the temerity to turn round and accuse the Elizabethans of treating women as commercial objects!

The play presents to us three women—Bianca, the widow and Kate—in their social, economic and marital aspects. To take Bianca first: she begins as if butter wouldn't melt in her mouth:

> Sir, to your pleasure humbly I subscribe . . .

But beneath the velvet voice there are nerves of steel; and the humble submissive Bianca turns out to be such a scheming, manipulative scholar that she twists her two young tutors round her little fingers, deftly playing one against the other, so that the romantic comedy of love is swamped by the farce of the intrigue:

> I'm no breeching scholar in the schools
> I'll not be tied to hours nor pointed times,
> But learn my lessons as I please myself.

And please herself she does; she schemes and plots with master and servant behind her father's back, and actually consents to a secret wedding which is arranged by clever servants. So much so, when confronted by the irate father, all that Lucentio/Cambio can do is to confess sheepishly:

> Love wrought these Miracles.

Miracles?—intrigues, deceptions, elopement would be better chosen terms.

The dull suitor Hortensio learns his lesson too; shocked and horrified by Bianca's flirtatious ways, he makes his decision:

> . . . I will be married to a wealthy widow
> Ere three days pass, which hath as long loved me
> As I have loved this proud disdainful haggard.

Proud, disdainful haggard, to wit, an untamed female hawk; and we are not talking about curst, shrewd Kate, but her beautiful, mild sister. Let us note too, that for every tamed woman, there are two let loose on an unsuspecting male population.

We are informed forthwith that Hortensio has hastened to Petruchio's "taming school" so that he might be taught the tricks of the trade "to tame a shrew and charm her chattering tongue." Sure enough, he is present on the stage throughout the two major scenes of Kate's taming; a gaping gawking, admiring spectator to Kate's tantrums and her husband's peccadilloes. He is supposed to be learning all the time and at the end of it all, he is ready to take on the world, leave alone his widow:

> Well Petruchio, this has put me in heart
> Have to my widow, and if she be forward
> Then hast thou taught Hortensio untoward.

Brave words indeed! To wit, Petruchio's demonstration on taming a wife is likely to prove unlucky for any wife who proposes to be perverse. But as we realize with glee, "taming" is not *that* simple a process—bullying, starving, raving, ranting and browbeating a woman into submission. The widow has the last laugh on Hortensio; at the final banquet she is loud, opinionated, and worst of all, rude to a member of her own sex. Kate responds to her mean taunts with great restraint and dignity. And when poor Hortensio "entreats" her to come to him, the widow's answer is:

> She will not come; she bids you to come to her.

What then, how then, why then? Is there no such thing as a foolproof taming process that one can apply to all women? Are some men better tamers than others? How is it that in a play that started with one shrew we are left with two whose shrewishness we didn't even suspect in the first place?

The answer to these questions would entail that we change our mindset and stop thinking simplistically about "taming" and "shrews." I have tried to show all along that simplistic notions of Love, Life and Money are no help when we deal with Shakespeare—and perish the thought that an early comedy is a second-rate play. As I approach the end of my paper, let me put my thoughts across to you as precisely as I can:

Taming is an offensive phrase—and the suggestion of hawks, falcons and sundry other animals does not help matters. But if we look closely at Petruchio's treatment of Kate, we may observe the following:

1. He is no ordinary mercenary who is out to win a wealthy wife. There is romance, excitement, wildness and adventure in his colourful background:

> Have I not in my time heard lions roar?
> Have I not heard the sea, puffed up with winds,
> Rage like an angry boar chafed with sweat?
>
> Have I not heard great ordnance in the field
> And Heaven's artillery thunder in the skies?

If one stretches one's imagination a little, this is just the kind of background that Othello came from—that so charmed Desdemona.

2. He comes prepared to appreciate her strength of character and her resistance. He is delighted and amused to hear that she has broken her lute over his hapless friend Hortensio's head:

   Now by the world, it is a lusty wench;
   I love her ten times more than e'er I did!

   Ignore the "love" and the tremendous "attraction" behind the taming—and one loses what is best in the play!
3. Modern scholars have been quick to point out that the strategies behind the "taming" are in fact psychological[2]:

   Kate, the prettiest Kate in the Christendom
   Kate of Kate Hall, my super-dainty Kate . . .
   Take this of me, Kate of my consolation;
   Hearing thy mildness praised in every town
   Thy virtues spoke of, and thy beauty sounded
   Yet not so deeply as to thee belongs,
   Myself am moved to woo thee for my wife.

   He presents an image of her as the world would want her to be:

   'T was told me you were rough and coy and sullen
   And now I find report a very liar,
   For thou art pleasant, gamesome, passing courteous
   But slow in speech, yet sweet as springtime flowers.

   Her temperament is summed up in *ironic inversions*, and he "opposes reality with created fiction. (Brian Morris). He provokes her to take another look at herself—at the shrewishness which she has perhaps built up as a defensive technique.
4. He matches her high spirits, quick wit, intelligence and repartee with his own. Charismatic, sublimely confident and totally in control of the situation, he is in every way her match—a refreshing change from the dull, colourless Gremios, Hortensios and the passing Lucentios with the likes of whom Padua is cluttered.
5. We must note that he offers her no violence; whip-cracking,

slapping Petruchios who push their Kates around are un-Shakespearean aberrations. It is she who strikes him to which his response is: (and we must imagine the steel in the voice and the spark in the eye)

> I swear I'll cuff you if you strike again.

But the fact is he doesn't.

6. As for the apparent humiliation and shame that is heaped on Kate before the wedding ceremony—his outlandish clothes and his outrageous behaviour are meant to bring home to her, her own disgraceful unpreparedness for the solemn contract of marriage. By something akin to a technique of displacement he shows that his dreadful clothes are akin to the assumed self she has put on—the disgraceful curst behaviour that she constantly sports. As the wily Tranio is quick to perceive:

   > He hath some meaning in his mad attire.

   The truth is Kate has never seen herself as others see her—and Petruchio burlesques her unreasonable conduct—shouting, bullying, slapping the priest, even as she has kicked, screamed, slapped and broken people's heads. What he offers her is an image of herself—which could also act as a treatment.
7. If inversion and displacement are used at first, dislocation of normality is what he uses after the wedding. He exposes her to the realities of hunger and cold even while he shows her the entire domestic world of servants, cooks, suppers, servicemen, carpets, trenchers, cups—which she will have to organize and manage. Refreshingly realistic, he introduces her to cook, groom, haberdasher and tailor, dragging marital love out of its remote poetic perch in the heavens, bringing it down to earth where real life is. Kate is taught to mind her manners, say thank you—for where is it said that a spirited intelligent woman can do without her manners? And all along she is given valuable lessons on how to control her servants (not by kicking, slapping or bullying), how to manage her household and conduct her social relationships. And so, by the time they set out for Padua, her only recourse is to acquiesce in his every whim:

> Then God be blessed, it is the blessed son
> But sun it is not, when you say it is not,
> And the moon changes even as your mind;
> What you will have it named, even that it is
> And so it shall be for Katherine!

Even while we recognize Petruchio's triumph, we regret that the fight is over. But it is not abject surrender. When confronted by old Vincentio and told to greet him as a young and fresh gentlewoman—this is how the great Shakespearean actress Peggy Ashcroft played Kate. She froze, stared in horror, first at the old man and then at her husband—and then rolled with laughter as the joke dawned on her at last. She can hardly contain her mirth as she addresses the old man:

> Young budding virgin, fair, fresh and sweet
> Whither away, where is thy abode?

To this perversely Petruchio responds:

> Why, how now Kate, I hope thou are not mad,
> This is a man, old, wrinkled, faded, withered
> And not a maiden, as thou say'st he is.

And this time, wiping away the tears of laughter, she rises to the occasion splendidly:

> Pardon, old father, my mistaking eyes
> That have been so bedazzled with the sun . . .

Indeed, great Shakespearean actresses from Peggy Ashcroft to the very feminist and Marxist Vanessa Redgrave agree that the key to playing this energetic, vivacious and lively Shakespearean heroine successfully is to realize that she falls in love with her madcap ruffian somewhere along the way. The games people play in their complex social inter-relationship is a peculiar game indeed—and it takes two to play any game. Kate has now understood the rules of the game that her husband is playing—she will learn it so well that she will shortly beat him at his own game.

Which brings us back to where we started: by the time Kate is summoned so arbitrarily by her husband, she has learnt patience, tact, self-control and caring for others.

> Katherine, that cap of yours becomes you not.
> Off with that bauble, throw it underfoot.

This can be public degradation or a private joke between husband and wife who understand each other very well. And Petruchio's invitation to her to deliver her final speech is tactful:

> Tell these headstrong women
> What duty they do owe to their lords and husbands.

Not what you owe to your lord and husband—he is in fact, giving her the freedom to reply to the women who have insulted her and humiliated her:

> Fie, fie, unknit that threatening unkind brow
> And dart not scornful glances from those eyes.

Northrop Frye makes a very pertinent observation: "When we first see Katherine, she is bullying Bianca, and when we take leave of her, she is still bullying Bianca, but she has learnt how to do it with social approval on her side."

> Thy husband is thy lord, thy life, thy keeper
> Thy head, thy sovereign: one that cares for thee
> And for thy maintenance commits his body
> To painful labour both by sea and land . . .
> Whilst thou liest warm at home, secure and safe.

"The past," writes L.P.Hartley, "is another country. They do things differently there." We are talking here about an age when the woman's domain was the home; it was the menfolk who were exposed to all the hazards of life by sea or land.

> And craves no other tribute at thy hands

But love, fair looks and true obedience.

What is suggested is a sort of quid pro quo—a return or exchange that suited social roles and functions as they existed then.

Such duty as the subject owes the prince
Even such, a woman oweth to her husband;

(She is quoting the Bishop's Bible here.)

I am ashamed that women are so simple
To offer war where they should kneel for peace;
Or seek for rule, supremacy and sway
When they are bound to serve, love and obey.

Abject, unconditional surrender? Male chauvinism doing its worst in a patriarchal society? An intelligent, spirited woman, tamed, broken by marriage? It is not Kate's spirit that is broken, only her pride and arrogance. Let me quote the feminist whom I admire the most—Germaine Greer. "The submission of a woman like Kate is genuine and exciting, because she has something to lay down, her pride and individuality. . . . Kate's speech at the close of the play is the greatest defence of Christian monogamy ever written. It rests upon the role of a husband as protector and friend, and it is valid because Kate has found a man who is capable of being both. . . Shakespeare recognized marriage as a difficult state of life, requiring discipline, energy, mutual respect and great forbearance."[3]

Just to keep the gender balance right I would like to quote a male critic as well—Harold Goddard, who regards male superiority as a "wholly unshakespearean" doctrine. "The play is an early version of *What Every Woman Knows*—what every woman knows, being of course that the woman can lord it over her man as long as she allows him to think that he is lording it over her."[4] Goddard is of course being more Catholic than the Pope—more feminist than the feminists.

There is no simple answer to the question: What did Shakespeare think of men and women? And about the relationships between them? A sensible answer would seem to be, as Harriet

Hawkins suggests: "It takes all kinds to make a world." It is absurd to suggest that there is only one kind of woman or two kinds of women—or indeed that there is only one set of criteria by which the women in Shakespeare's plays may be judged. If Lear says of Cordelia

> Her voice was ever soft and low
> An excellent thing in woman

we will do well to remember that his best heroines talk nineteen to the dozen, while the men are bedazzled by their verbal brilliance. And in all fairness it must be stated that *The Taming of the Shrew* is the only Shakespearean comedy in which the woman is re-educated; in all the rest it is the man.

NOTES

1. See S. Schoenbaum, *Shakespeare's Lives* (Oxford, 1970), pp. 40-42.
2. See the Introduction to the Arden Text, ed. Brian Morris (London, 1981), p. 107.
3. *The Female Eunuch* (New York, 1971), pp. 220-21.
4. *The Meaning of Shakespeare* (Chicago,1951), vol. 1, pp. 68 ff.

Profit and Delight:
The Plays of Ben Jonson

K. VENKATA REDDY

The function of the English drama was traditionally didactic. Drama, after all, was brought into being only because it seemed, more than any other existing genre, an effective method of preaching to the people. The "ostensible purpose of dramatic production remained didactic to the end of the Medieval drama. Now the end of the Medieval drama almost coincided with the culmination of the Renaissance drama."[1]

That Jonson was not content with his early attempts to combine didactic and comic elements is evident from the change of his dramatic technique in every one of his first five comedies. From the composition of *The Case is Altered* (1597) to the completion of *Volpone* (1605), Jonson's comedies, we may say, are experimental. In no single comedy before *Volpone* is Jonson able to achieve his object of the fusion of the didactic and the comic. Either the satiric and didactic material is overshadowed by the comic as in *The Case is Altered,* or the didactic material overshadows and almost obscures the comic material as in *Every Man out of His Humour.*

Of Jonson's early plays, only *A Tale of a Tub* and *The Case is Altered* are extant. *A Tale of a Tub*, unacknowledged by Jonson, was written without any didactic or satiric content.[2] It is in *The Case is Altered* that Jonson made an effort to divert his comedy towards didactic ends. Nevertheless, it is primarily a romantic comedy and the didactic content is quite subsidiary The exposure of the follies of the gallants, Onion and Juniper, is, no doubt, laughable but it lacks any great didactic value. If the satire is embedded in the boisterous exuberance in which the play is steeped, it is lost in light and funny conversation. Avarice, embodied in Jaques de Price is, no doubt, an excellent vice for moralistic treatment. But there is little stress on the social effects of his avarice. Moreover, most of the scenes in which the miser appears are more comic than didactic. On the whole, the atmosphere of the play lacks moral consciousness.[3]

In *Every Man in His Humour*, Jonson begins to combine a considerable amount of satire with his comedy. He attacks the false social values by which the fashionable and would-be-fashionable gallants regulate their conduct. Through Matthew, Stephen and Bobadill, he parodies the elaborate terminology associated with fencing (I.iii.184-229; II.iii.123-53), hawking (I.i.28-56), quarrelling (I.i.86-110; III.ii.107-15; iv.145-59). He ridicules the poor literary taste of pretenders to fashion (I.iii.66-70; 125-52; III.iv.22-102). Thus the action of the play is designed to exhibit the fatuities, the follies, the obsessions, the pretensions, and the absurdities of the different characters. The more serious threats to society—the breakdown in communication between generations (Knowells) and between husband and wife (Kitelys)—are eventually dissipated through the timely intervention of Justice Clement. And though the play "concludes amid reconciliation, rejoicing and communal festivities, there remains the realization that were it not for the fateful, ordering presence of Doctor Clement, the follies would have continued and developed into serious social problems."[4]

However, at least half of the play is concerned with non-satiric matter,[5] and even the satire the play contains is light as most of the material on the follies of the gallants is comic. The oaths of Bobadill, the sword-play of Matthew and Bobadill (I.iii.195-229), and the argument over the virtues and evils of tobacco (III.ii.107-16)—all this is essentially theatrical stuff, causing a great deal of amusement to the audience. Jonson, however, has given so much of importance to wit and humour in *Every Man in His Humour* that his didactic purpose is pushed to the background. This he may well have realized, perhaps, to his great dissatisfaction.

The result is a radical change of technique in the immediately following play, *Every Man out of His Humour*. The satiric and didactic material does no longer take a secondary place in this play which is moralistic to the core. The moral purpose is to make men "fit for fair societies" by giving them "pills to purge" them of their shallowness and of their false social values.

The didactic material is embodied in the main characters—Fastidius Briske, Fungoso and Sogliardo. Fastidius, who is an adept in the art of speaking always of his friendships with the great, is purged of his folly when he is confronted with the severe punishment of confinement in a debtors' prison. He then cries "O, heaven." Fungoso, who is a blind imitator of Fastidius, is finally cured of his delusions and resolves never to imitate

> any more gallants either in purse, or apparel, but as shall become a gentleman, for good carriage, or so. (V.ix.3-5)

Sogliardo, who is prepared to buy the name of a gentleman, is finally exposed as

> A swine without a head, without braine, wit, any thing, indeed, ramping to gentilitie. (III.iv.65-66)

and is snatched out of his folly.

It is now manifest that Jonson's primary purpose in the creation of these characters is didactic rather than dramatic. Their portrayal is expository rather than theatrical. The shallow characters talk of their follies or display them rather than enact them. On the whole, the play is overweighted by matter. Jonson's dramatic sense is almost overshadowed by his intense desire to include didactic satire in the play.

It is in *Volpone* that Jonson demonstrated his didactic and comic techniques in their maturity. The experimental devices of the previous 'comical satires' are here eschewed. There is no chorus, Asper or Crites, here to explain the didactic function. The satire is implicit. The morality is pervasive but the moral accent is never distinctly or separately heard. It only qualifies the value of every note. Jonson's moral purpose in *Volpone* is

> to informe yong-men to all good disciplines, inflame grownemen to all great vertues, keepe old-men in their best and supreme state. (Dedication, ll.24-26)

With his earnest purpose "to inform men in the best reason of liuing,' Jonson builds the play on the power of wealth and its repercussions. Almost every scene is so designed as to exhibit the repercussions of wealth, the insolence which it breeds and the infamies which are committed for excessive love of it. In short, *Volpone* is a powerful picture of moral depravity of the age.

Volpone is the embodiment of lust for sensual pleasures. Wealth is his instrument. The legacy hunters—Voltore, Corbaccio and Carvino, the birds of prey—are motivated entirely by greed. Blinded by inordinate avarice for wealth, Corvino condescends to procure his own innocent wife, Corbaccio disinherits his own son by declaring him to be a bastard and Voltore perjures himself twice in the open court. "Society may depend upon its Moscas to outwit its Corbaccios, its Voltores, and its Corvinos, but it can only wait for the Moscas and the Volpones to betray themselves."[6] The denouement is brought about through Mosca's own greed. Volpone, Mosca and the three legacy hunters are duly punished. Celia who is resistant to vice and Bonario who rescues Celia are saved. Though for the time being these two virtuous characters suffer, ultimately they are rewarded and vice is worsted. The play closes on a didactic note:

> Let all, that see these vices thus rewarded,
> Take heart, and loue to study 'hem. Mischiefes feed
> Like beasts, till they be fat, and then they bleed.
>
> (V.xii.149-51)

Volpone provides as much delight as profit. Nevertheless, it is often said to be too forbidding a play to provide any amusement. "If Jonson ever sports here," we are told, "it is in the sombre and lurid fashion of his own 'sporting Kyd.' . . . The air is heavy and fetid with moral disease."[7] "The satirical intensity," says Gregory Smith, "rarely, if ever, permits that laughter at vice."[8] We cannot possibly fall in line with these views. Because, we know that Jonson meant *Volpone* to be a merry comedy. The last lines of his Prologue announce his goal:

> All gall, and compresse, from his inke he drayneth,

Onely, a little salt remayneth;
Wherewith, he'll rub your cheeks, til (red with laughter)
They shall looke fresh, a weeke after. (II.33-36)

And there is every reason to suppose that Dryden would have included *Volpone* when he wrote: "To make men appear pleasantly ridiculous on the stage was his talent. . . . That Ben Jonson's plays were pleasant, he must want reason who denies."[9]

Volpone is not, in any case, a too forbidding play. It does provide plenty of fun, mirth and innocent laughter. The play bubbles over with what may be called sardonic humour. Almost every scene is larded with dramatic poetry that is constantly imaginative, comic, and exciting. The comic phase of *Volpone* has not received the due attention because laughter is so integral a part of the terrible portrayal of greed that the reader is likely to overlook the variety of theatrical and ironic laughter. Also, the comic material of *Volpone* is such that it requires visual representation on the stage for its fullest expression and appeal.

The play is replete with a variety of comic scenes. Apart from the comic treatment of the gulls, "the gigs of Nano, Castrone and Androgyno, the mountebank scenes, and the action of Sir Politique and Lady Would-be consume some 900 lines out of 2400, or almost 38% of the first four acts."[10] The scenes in which the legacy hunters appear to make their respective offerings to the magnifico and discover how bad his health is, are full of good theatrical stuff. Voltore's pompous affability and self-complacent credulity render his folly laughable. Assured by Mosca that he is the sole heir to Volpone's property, he bursts out in childish glee:

Happy, happy, me!
By what good chance, sweet Mosca?
MOS. Your desert, Sir;
I know no second cause.
VOLT. Thy modestie
Is loth to know it: well we shall requite it. (I.iii.47-49)

Corbaccio is very funny. Reassured by Mosca of his succession to Volpone's riches, he croaks his joy at the imminence of

Volpone's death and his prospective wealth. We cannot but laugh when such an old creature says:

> I may ha' my youth restor'd to me, why not? (I.iv.129)

Next comes the "witty merchant" Corvino. It is amusing to watch Mosca overcome Corvino's prudence and spur him into shouting stupid insults into Volpone's ear.

Then, the fantastic creatures—Nano, Androgyno and Castrone, whom Volpone maintains for his amusement make a good deal of comic appeal. The mountebank scene in which Volpone with "a starched beard" and "an old tilt-feather" sells patent medicine is out and out comic. Above all, the voluptuous visions which Volpone paints before the eyes of the distracted Celia are a provocation to the senses. Then, the last scene in which Voltore falls down on the floor pretending that he is possessed by a devil under the delusion that he will surely, in this manner, win Volpone's favour, is quite hilarious. All this suggests that the effect of the play is far from that of tragic foreboding.

However, *Volpone* marks a crucial phase of Jonson's development as a comic dramatist. The success of *Volpone* seems to have alleviated Jonson's bitterness over the failure of Sejanus and the three unsuccessful attempts to bring about a harmonious fusion of 'profit and delight.' Naturally his mood is relaxed. Besides, as his powers of realistic depiction have come into full play, his loudly proclaimed moral purposes are subdued. He now seems to concur with Shakespeare and Donne that good and evil, in this world, are matters of opinion. So to Jonson mankind is subdivided, it now seems, not into good and bad men but into rogues and fools. Consequently, he seems to feel that his role as a comic playwright is not to judge but to observe. Therefore we may say with Harry Levin that after *Volpone* "Jonson's genius underwent a metempsychosis of its own and, having died with a stern satirist, was reborn in a genial observer."[11]

The Alchemist is built on the double theme of lust and greed. The profession of alchemy at once notorious and obscure with its mountebank practices and its mystic pretensions, the most picturesque of social pestilences, was a matter best fitted to furnish forth the cosmos of Jonsonian typical comedy. The purpose of the play is the shaming of a variety of gulls victimized by the charlatan philosophy of the day, thereby hoping to "better men." The confederate swindlers, Subtle, Face and Dol Common bait and dupe Dapper, Drugger and Sir Epicure Mammon. The mere expectation of plentiful gold and the very sight of a lady enraptures Sir Epicure. Dapper and Drugger are lured by the prospects of easy money. Tribulation and Ananias, the hypocritical puritans, are overjoyed at the prospect of possessing gold. But, by dazzling their victims with a show of infinite riches and by exploiting their greed, the three partners cheat the gulls of their money. Jonson thus shows how the desire to become suddenly rich brings people into the sharper's clutches. While exposing contemporary phase of imposture and its corresponding credulity, Jonson, in *The Alchemist*, paints a picture which remains true to the permanent acts of human roguery and weakness.

Though soaked in satire, *The Alchemist* is not without its comic purpose. Just as the satiric is ingeniously woven into the purely comic world of *Epicoene*, the comic is adroitly introduced into the satiric world of *The Alchemist*, testifying to the fact that

> When the wholesome remedies are sweet, . . .
> in their working, gaine, and profit meet. (Prologve, ll.15-16)

As Anne Barton rightly observes, *The Alchemist* is "The funniest play Jonson ever wrote, the most cunning in its marriage of erudition with brilliant theatricality."[12] It stands out from the rest of his work for the number of bizarre and hilarious stage situations it invents. We thoroughly enjoy the dramatic situations in which Dapper is blindfolded being pinched by Face and Subtle and Surly is trapped in his Spanish disguise. The audience also derive pleasure in the simulated prostration of the two charlatans, Subtle and Face, when the laboratory blows up off-stage, their real panic when Lovewit unexpectedly returns from his hop-fields or the innocent salutations of Ananias just at the moment when that household has exploded into a pitched battle.

In this essentially artistic play, the comic is ingrained in the very ingenuity of the plot, the liveliness of the action and the delightful delineation of manners. The satire unfailingly flavours the fun without destroying it. Laughter and delight are wrought into the composition of Dol, Face and Subtle, but the satiric, ironic quality is also there. They are shown on more than one level, as rogues, as insects or animals, and as higher beings, that they and others think they are. The simultaneous existence of multiple levels "helps create some of the humour and much of the irony which gather about a whore who thinks of herself as a 'republiqe,' a quack who will 'thunder' a man in pieces, and a pander who wears a uniform and calls himself 'Captaine.'"[13] Hence it is as difficult to isolate the comic and the didactic in these characters as in that of the wife of Bath or in that of the boisterous rogues in *The Beggar's Opera*. Thus, *The Alchemist* yields a world of profit and delight.

To sum up, with a growing sense of urgency to include in his comedy the philosophic material which should eternize it, Jonson switched over from the easy-moving, and light-hearted plays—*The Case is Altered* and *Every Man in His Humour*—to *Every Man out of His Humour* and *Cynthia's Revels* for a better integration of character and action with the moral purpose, and succeeded only partially. But with Poetaster, to some degree, and with *Volpone*, *Epicoene*, *The Alchemist* and *Bartholomew Fair* consummately, he outgrew the heavy sententiousness of his "Comicall Satyres." Jonson's diminishing emphasis on punishment of folly is clearly discerned in his mature plays except, of course, in *Volpone*. For, as moral attitudes become more closely integrated with artistic forms in these plays, "punishment serves increasingly as emotional resolution rather than as the execution of strict justice."[14] This is the finally arrived method of Jonson, the serious moral realist and the comic artist.

Thus, Jonson succeeded well in his dogged determination to make comedy convey serious thought as well as serious laughter thereby achieving a harmonious fusion of "profit and delight." Comedy in his hands becomes a perfect communication between the author and the audience. Jonson, like Shaw later on, seeks to teach through pleasurable means right values of life. But, in doing so, he is not concerned with narrow morality or petty rules of conduct. It is not as though he was a doughty champion of didacticism. He is by no means a conventional moralist. The material of his plays is derived not from any abstract heights of theology but from the matter which interests him personally. Also, his treatment of good and evil and of social and economic problems in his plays is based not so much on the ethics of his own and preceding ages as on what he himself considers to be good and evil. Moreover, his failure. to mete out poetic justice to the miser in *The Case is Altered*; to censure the rogues in *Every Man in His Humour* and in *The Alchemist*, to give anything but sympathetic portrayals of low-life characters in *Bartholomew Fair*, and to preach sermons on drunkenness is enough to indicate that he is more interested in achieving dramatic effects than in punishing the evil. It is now clear that Jonson's is essentially a comic dramatist using the didactic theory for literary and dramatic purposes.

NOTES

1. David Klein, *Literary Criticism from the Elizabethan Dramatists* (New York, 1910), p. 3.
2. *A Tale of a Tub*, originally written in 1596-97, was revised and licensed only on May 7, 1633. It is when Jonson finally revised the comedy that he inserted satiric material. This is made clear from the allusions in the play to Inigo Jones.
3. It is not for nothing that Jonson discarded *The Case is Altered* altogether later. The seeds of his discard undoubtedly lay in his lack of enthusiasm for romantic comedy as a medium for didactic material.
4. Lawrence L. Levin, "Clement Justice in *Every Man in His Humour*," *SEL*, XII (Spring 1972), p. 307.
5. See Elizabeth Woodbridge's chart of the amount of space devoted to humorous characters in *Every Man in His Humour*, which gives an estimate of the satiric material. (*Studies in Jonson's Comedy*, pp. 51-53).
6. W. Speed Hill, "Biography, Autobiography, and *Volpone*," *SEL*, XII (Spring 1972), p. 328.
7. Herford and Simpson, vol. II, p. 55.
8. Gregory Smith, *Ben Jonson* (London: Macmillan, 1919), p. 110.
9. *Essays of John Dryden*, ed. W.P. Ker, vol. I, pp. 138-39.
10. Ralph Nash, "The Comic Intent of *Volpone*," *SP*, XLIV (Jan. 1947), p. 38.

11. Harry Levin, "Jonson's Metempsychosis," *PQ*, XXII (July 1943), p. 239.
12. Anne Barton, *Ben Jonson, Dramatist* (New York: Cambridge University Press, 1984), p. 142.
13. Edward B. Partridge, *The Broken Compass* (London: Chatto and Windus, 1958), p. 120.
14. William W.E. Slights, "*Epicoene* and the Prose Paradox," *PQ*, XLIX (April 1970), p. 187.

Sheridan's *The School for Scandal* as High Comedy

SHARAD GADEKAR

High Comedy is largely concerned with social education of both old and young through their own and others' mistakes learning even to laugh at themselves. One of the greatest ambitions of many people in society is to be accepted in society—to 'arrive'—to know the language and manner of the in-group. These people are ever ready to find their role in the gatherings of the social group. There, they will hear both casual gossip and public comment on everything from current fashion and human behaviour to the latest trends and institutions and ideas. It is no wonder, therefore, that several high comedies have been called 'schools'—*The School for Husbands, The School for Wives* and *The School for Scandal*.

The high comedy of wit and manners is a comedy of correction, a civilizing force for humanity. A truly civilized society exists only where women freely participate as equals of men, adding the essential warmth to intellectual discussion and permitting both men and women the impersonal appreciation of the opposite sex. Likewise, high comedy, the most civilized of comic forms, did not develop until women became important as characters. The civil world of high comedy can be considered as belonging to two types—the 'social' and the 'individual.' The first type deals with social affairs in which the characters try to be conspicuous in society. The characters enjoy the social games. The second type has characters who, by virtue of their individualities, carve out an independent existence. In the plots of such comedies, experienced adults pick their way skilfully and confidently among the pitfalls of a complex social world, maintaining their individuality while outwardly conforming to the expectations of the group.

Every high comedy has its share of fops and faddish fools who think themselves in fashion, when they merely reflect the surface manners of the tyrant group. English high comedy of the seventeenth and eighteenth centuries delighted in labelling such characters with appropriately laughable names—Sir Novelty Fashion, Lady Would-be, Sir Fopling Flutter, Mrs. Betty Modish and the like.

In the seventeenth century, in France, Moliere, who drew many of his plots from Plautus, but unlike Plautus, has at the centre of his plays women of wit and sense to provide variety, complexity and a high touch of teasing that moves the play towards the civility of high comedy. Moliere moved all the way into high comedy in *The Misanthrope*. Here, an adult couple, free from all restrictions explores their social relationships with other free adults. Celimene keeps herself at the centre of a circle of adoring beaux through caustic wit and malicious character-sketches of all her friends. The overly frank Alceste, the misanthrope of the play, falls in love with her, but objects to her befriending people with whom she finds so much fault and to her obvious enjoyment of the social group. When Celimene is finally trapped in her own hypocrisy, they separate for ever, unable to achieve a workable relationship.

Before Moliere, Shakespeare had tried to score a point in *Much Ado About Nothing*. Beatrice and Benedick are about to destroy a fragile relationship because they are so determined to be witty that their friends bring out sonnets each has written declaring their mutual love. Benedick, caught in the tangle of his own wit, confesses, "A miracle! here's our own hands against our hearts. Come, I will have thee." Yet, he cannot resist one last crack: "But, by this light, I take thee for pity."

Still another delight of comedy depends on disillusionment, a full awareness of human limitations, as Louis Kronenberger says in *The Thread of Laughter*: "Comedy is always jarring us with the evidence that we are no better than other people, and always comforting with the knowledge that other people are no better than we. It makes us more critical but at last leaves us more tolerant."

The progress towards high comedy in one form or another continued till we arrive at Etherege's *The Man of Mode* (1678) in which we meet Dorimant, the first fully developed hero of Restoration Comedy, who samples casual sexual relations insisting on freedom and variety because he is destined eventually for someone, who is not so casual. One mistress tries to hold him by his vows of love, but he casts her off with indignant irony: "Constancy at my years! . . . Youth has a long journey to go, madam; should I have set up my rest at the first inn I lodged at, I should never have arrived at the happiness I now enjoy." William Congreve's heroine in *The Way of the World* voices a similar view: "Why, one makes lovers as fast as one pleases, and they live as long as one pleases, and they die as soon as one pleases; and then, if one pleases one makes more."

The most famous stage duelists in love are Sir Peter Teazle and Lady Teazle in Sheridan's *The School for Scandal* (1777) created more than a century after the Restoration. English high comedy was largely superseded by sentimental comedy. With the pragmatism of nineteenth century scientific and industrial growth and the rise of the middle class, it seemed destined to disappear altogether. However, in the 1890s, Oscar Wilde, reacting against pragmatism and scientific determinism, briefly popularized a high comedy which explored characters trying to live life as though it were art. The crowning achievement of Wilde's Art for Art's Sake drama is *The Importance of Being Earnest* (1895). A young country gentleman, Jack Worthing, escapes his duties and responsibilities of raising a young ward by inventing a callous young brother named Earnest, to court Jack's attractive young ward. For the characters in the play, lying becomes an art. Jack learns that he is the long-lost cousin of the girl he wants to marry, that the best friend who has shared his escapades is really his younger brother, and most ironically, that his name actually is, Earnest! He confesses to his intended: "It is a terrible thing for a man to find out suddenly that all his life he has been speaking nothing but the truth."

After Wilde, we have G.B. Shaw's special blending of high comedy with the social, 'problem play.' Shaw widened its scope beyond the personal relationships of lovers, parents and friends, to show characters involved in social, political and philosophical problems. Even a secondary character like Violet, in *Man and Superman* won't let her young man defy his wealthy father by acknowledging her as his wife: "We can't afford it. . . . You can be as romantic as you please about love, Hector, but mustn't be romantic about money."[1]

George Meredith, in a classic essay on "The Idea of Comedy" defines 'high comedy' as "that which evokes thoughtful laughter from spectators who remain emotionally detached from the action, the folly, pretentiousness and incongruity in human behaviour." Meredith finds its highest form within the Comedy of Manners, the more graceful, urbane and witty sort of comedy. Its shafts are driven by the bow of the intellect, with verbal play, often deft repartee, and mental agility. High Comedy, when it deals with deft minds, often shows them at work to satisfy the desires of their bodies. The purpose of high comedy is not, consciously, moralistic, though serious purpose is often implicit in the satire frequently present in it. The true employment of high comedy demands a certain intellectual effort and philosophical detachment on the part of the audience. In neo-classical times, a criterion for high comedy was its appeal to and reflection of 'higher' social class and its observance of decorum, as illustrated in Congreve's plays.

To turn to *The School for Scandal*.[2] Wit in its various aspects seeks to heighten the play's comic element. The word 'wit' has a number of distinct, though related, meanings. The oldest meaning is identical with 'mind' as in Wycliffe's translation of the Bible: "Who knew the wit of the Lord." Another long-established meaning is, 'a faculty of the mind.' This is still in use when we speak of someone having 'lost his wits.' We observe this in *The School for Scandal* (II.i) in the dialogue between Sir Peter Teazle and Lady Teazle. We also observe equality between men and women in intellectual discussion, permitting both men and women the impersonal appreciation of the opposite sex. A form of attack through mockery may exist in any literary medium but is often regarded as a medium in itself. Satire, which is a manifestation of wit, has its origin in the Latin word 'satura,' a vessel filled with the earliest agricultural produce of the year used in seasonal festival, to celebrate harvest. A secondary meaning is 'miscellany of entertainment,' implying merry-making at such festivals, probably, including verbal duels. This kind of duel can be seen in Act II, Scene 1 and Act IV, Scene 3, the latter in the Screen Scene where Lady Teazle says: "My extravagance! I'm sure, I'm not more extravagant than a woman of fashion ought to be."

Wit is also a significant characteristic of high comedy. It can be defined as a literary form which constitutes a comic imitation of a serious literary form. *The School for Scandal* can be seen as an imitation of a serious work. We have in the Screen Scene, Charles Surface selling everything to his disguised uncle except the latter's picture, saying, "Odd's heart, no more I can—nor with gravity either." Also, as is common in old husband/young wife plots, Sir Peter Teazle, cautiously, chose a woman from the country, expecting simplicity and gratitude. But his caution was wasted as seen from his utterance: "It's now six months since Lady Teazle made me happiest of men—and I have been the miserablest dog ever since that committed wedlock!—Now she plays her part in all the extravagant fopperies and fashions of the town as if she had seen a bush or a grassplot."

Likewise, the young wife chose the old husband to escape the boredom of country living, where her daily occupation was "to inspect the dairy, superintend the poultry, make extracts from the family receipt-book and comb my aunt Deborah's lap dog." Her situation was "a very disagreeable one, or I should never have married you." Yet, for all his anger, Sir Peter will remain a comic victim of a teasing wife.

Sheridan, intricately, weaves several plots into a series of skirmishes of wit and ironic delight. At last, the whole entanglement comes to a head in one of the most famous scenes of comic irony, the Screen Scene. When the play was first performed, it was said to have exceeded "anything in living memory." "Not until the time of Wilde and Shaw was such comedy to be seen again in the English theatre."[3] Byron paid a rich tribute to Sheridan the dramatist, his wit and intelligence, ten days after Sheridan's death: "When summer's day declines above the hills, so feels the fullness of our heart and eyes, when all the genius which can perish, dies. A mighty spirit is eclipsed, a power hath passed from day to darkness."[4]

NOTES

1. George Kernodle, et al, *Invitation to the Theatre* (1971), p.146.
2. P.B. Sheridan, *The School for Scandal* (Macmillan India, 1981).
3. Roger Londsdate, *The Penguin History of English Literature*, pp. 176-77.
4. *Ibid.*

The Proviso Scene in William Congreve's *The Way of the World*

SHILPA GAURI GANPULE

The Proviso Scene or the Bargaining Scene in *The Way of the World* is the best scene ever produced by William Congreve, the famous dramatist of the Restoration period. The scene between Mirabell and Millamant, which occurs in the Fourth Act of the play, conveys a serious meaning and significance under the garb of comic mockery. By defining marriage and by providing comic fun, it serves a dual purpose.

Due to its dramatic significance, the Proviso Scene has attracted the attention of many critics. For Dobree, it is "Congreve's contribution to the philosophy of love." (144) He further says that the Bargaining Scene gives "a vision of the conflict in all marriage, of the desire to maintain one's own personality fighting vainly with the desire to love wholeheartedly." (146) Holland states that Mirabell's contract with Millamant suggests "an ideal of balance between the social and personal aspects of marriage." (180) Sharma notes that the Proviso Scene "expresses in a comic way the quintessence of understanding which must exist between the gay and the wild couples if they wish to make a success of the state of matrimony which society forces upon them if they want to have the privilege of living with each other." (75)

Using the device of the Proviso Scene was a regular convention of the Restoration comedies. But the Proviso Scene in *The Way of the World* is drastically different from the earlier provisos. As Sharma says, "In many of the earlier plays it has been primarily her concern only, probably because she was not yet sure of her equality, and man simply agreed to those conditions, as if there was still something in his power to grant. But in *The Way of the World*, the conditions are laid down and accepted both by the gallant and the lady: a state of equality between the sexes has been taken for granted and assured for the future." (74) Moreover the Proviso Scene has an added social significance. In the contemporary Restoration society, marriages were arranged by the parents. The younger people had no freedom to choose their mates. Many a time the pair had never seen each other before marriage. Marriage for love was rare and love was not expected to come before marriage, but after it. So marriage was just a bargain, as Butler points out:

> Matrimony's but a bargain made
> To serve the Turns of Interest and Trade. (76)

The Proviso Scene in *The Way of the World* brings the lovers together to discuss the important topic of their marriage. With this scene, Congreve allows the lovers to develop a relation based on mutual understanding, which may help them to lead a happy and successful married life.

When the scene begins, Millamant states that she would like to be followed by her lover to the very last: "I'll fly and be followed to the last moment." She wants Mirabell to solicit her to the very last. She would not like to be "freed from the agreeable fatigues of solicitation." Millamant further declares that she would hate a lover who can live independently of his mistress even for a moment. She cannot tolerate the "pedantic arrogance" of the husband. She is not ready to marry unless and until she gets the surety of her will and pleasure: "I'll never marry unless I am first made sure of my will and pleasure." When Mirabell asks whether she would have both before marriage, Millamant answers that she will not give up her liberty even after marriage. She says, "I'll lie abed in morning as long as I please." Holland calls this a "significant expression of her narcisstic girlishness." (186) To this, Mirabell replies wittily, "then I'll get up in the morning as early as I please." Both these amusing views point out the wit and talent of both Mirabell and Millamant.

Millamant would not like to be called names after her marriage.

She would never like to be addressed as 'wife,' 'spouse,' 'my dear,' 'joy' 'jewel,' 'love,' 'sweetheart' etc. She considers it to be a "nauseous cant." She cannot bear her husband kissing her before folks. She would not like "to go to Hyde Park together the first Sunday in a chariot, to provoke eyes and whispers; and then never to be seen there together again; as if we were proud of one another the first week, and ashamed of one another ever after." She would not like to appear to be familiar with her husband. She remarks, "let us be as strange as if we had been married a great while, and as well-bred as if we were not married at all." Finally she says that she would visit anybody anytime. She would write letters to anybody and would wear clothes of her liking. She would be the sole empress of her tea-table and would like her husband to knock at the door whenever he comes in to meet her. Thus Millamant is quite straightforward and frank while setting forth her provisos.

Mirabell too has his own expectations from his wife. He also lays down certain conditions. He would not approve his wife sharing her secrets with her female friends, through whom she can go secretly to the theatre with a fop. He will not allow his wife to wear masks which are generally made of oiled-skins, hog-bones, hare's gall, pig-water and the marrow of a roasted cat. He also states that she should not wear tight dresses during her pregnancy because they will "mould my boy's head like a sugarloaf, and instead of a man-child, make me the father to a crooked billet." In this respect, Fujimura states, "Mirabell is probably the first True wit so sensible as to begin worrying about his offspring at the time he proposes to his mistress." (187) He also orders his wife not to take any alcoholic drinks.

Thus the Proviso Scene presents Mirabell and Millamant as witty persons. They both suit each other in brilliance of wit. Millamant expects wit in others, when she tells Petulant, "I wonder at the impudence of any illiterate Man, to offer to make love" and Mirabell definitely stands to her expectation in the Proviso Scene.

The Proviso Scene brings out a complete change in the personality of Millamant. Holland says, "it shows the enchanting Millamant brought from girlhood to maturity." (185) Before the Proviso Scene, Millamant treats love very lightly. Her use of love letters to pin up hair suggests her casual approach towards love.

She is happy in giving pain to her suitors. She mocks Marwood who has emotional involvement in her love affair. But after the proviso, we get a mature statement from Millamant: "Well, if Mirabell shou'd not make a good Husband, I am a lost Thing;—for I find I love him violently." Fujimura remarks, "Mrs. Millamant is better, however, when her real feelings come to the surface, and reveal her true nature, as a woman of sincerity and deep feeling, but, at the same time, a True wit with judgment and an awareness of decorum. This side of her is best demonstrated in the famous 'proviso' scene in which she capitulates to Mirabell." (190-91) But Holland thinks, "None of her feminist provisos deals with the personal aspects of marriage." They all, Mueschke points out, "are the result of her desire to prolong and increase her prenuptial glamour." (185) Holland further says that Millamant's provisos are developed femininely and that of Mirabell's in a masculine way. Mirabell's provisos begin with its imprimis or item. He starts by giving general instructions and then turns to the specific ones. Because of this Mueschke says that the wit of Mirabell is "predominantly judicial, that of Millamant is fanciful." (186)

The Proviso Scene also sheds light on the personality of Millamant. She is a True wit who is sincere, honest and never likes to keep facades. She wants to live an independent life. She would never accept life, dictated by her husband. She wants to retain her freedom even after marriage. She would never compromise with her convictions. At the same time Millamant maintains her innocence, her girlish immaturity when she expresses her expectation from her husband that he should follow her to the very last.

The Proviso Scene gives us the general principles on which a happy and ideal marriage is based. It announces the freedom and equality for both husband and wife. They should respect each other. They should have freedom of speech, action, and of taking decisions. As a well-bred and decent lady, Millamant considers Mirabell's conditions to be "horrid," since she would not have done any of the bad things, even though Mirabell had laid no conditions. Both Mirabell's and Millamant's expectations are worth considering.

The Proviso Scene gives the lovers an opportunity to understand their true nature. They throw away their masks and share their innermost thoughts, ideas, and feelings with each other. The Proviso Scene, in brief, foregrounds the true identity of both Mirabell and Millamant. Indeed it is one of the best scenes ever produced in the English drama.

Bibliography

Congreve, W. (1996) *The Way of The World.* Ed. C. Thomas. Madras: Macmillan.

Dobree, B. (1924) *Restoration Comedy.* London: Oxford University Press.

Holland, N. (1959) *The First Modern Comedies, The Significance of Etherege, Wycherley and Congreve.* Cambridge: Harvard University Press.

Fujimura, T. (1952) *The Restoration Comedy of Wit.* New Jersey: Princeton University Press.

Nicoll, A. (1925) *British Drama.* London: George G. Harrap.

Sharma, R. (1965) *Themes and Conventions in the Comedy of Manners.* Bombay: Asia.

Styan, J. (1996). *The English Stage, A History of Drama and Performance.* Cambridge: Cambridge University Press.

G.B. Shaw's *The Doctor's Dilemma*: A Problem Play

A.P. DANI

G. B. Shaw, the philosopher artist, declares in his *Preface* to *Pygmalion* that art should never be anything but didactic. He disapproves of popular art; he has no belief in popular religion and has no respect for popular heroics. To him, drama is no mere setting up of the camera to nature: it is the presentation in parable of the conflict between man's will and his environment: in a word, of problem. He has written plays with a deliberate intention of convincing the people of his opinion on social matters. Shaw, then, following Ibsen, has been a problem playwright.

The Doctor's Dilemma (1906) is a problem play. The basic problem in the play is: who is more valuable, a good man who has no genius or a man of genius who has no other goodness? However, Shaw avoids this central conflict in the play which has three sub-themes:

(a) the play is a satire on doctors, journalists and art-critics;
(b) it is Shaw's answer to the challenge that he could not write a play about death;
(c) it is dramatization of a brilliant short story about a middle-aged man who successfully murdered the husband of a woman with whom he had fallen in love, only to be disappointed in his purpose.

Due to the lack of concentration, the play has a diffuse structure. Sen Gupta believes that in the play Shaw "just skins over the real problem of poverty and disease and confines himself to be the explorer of trivialities." But to C.E.M. Joad, the problem is a real one. "If you can save only one man, do you choose an ordinary decent chap, upright and reliable but mediocre or an amoral egotist whose genius alone saves him from being a commonplace cad?" There is much to be said on either side.

For the ancient Greek philosophers, Goodness was an abstract virtue, yet in common human experience man or woman embodies Goodness without some qualification or dilution or blemish imposed by the limitations and inadequacies of human nature. Even a saint, a holy man, is only good within the limits he imposes upon himself by withdrawing from the total experience of human life. Our expectations of individual goodness have therefore to be narrowed down to some particular good or combination of particular goods. When Sir Colenso Ridgeon, in the play, faces the problem of this form, his decision is bound to be hampered by imperfect knowledge of the true nature of Goodness as it exists in the mind of God. It is beyond human power to achieve more than fragments of that total Goodness, and we cannot choose between two fragments. Though it is generally presumed that moral goodness is superior to artistic goodness, we cannot in any absolute sense know that it is so. It can be argued from both the sides. Great works of art influence multitudes of people through centuries while virtuous social conduct by any individual person may have only a narrowly limited and temporary influence. Nevertheless, if we were all great artists and at the same time all mean scoundrels (as Louis Dubedat in the play is) the world would be impossible to live in, for all social virtues would vanish; whereas if we were all virtuous within our narrow social environment (as Blenkinsop in the play is) the world would be at least tolerable, though without great art mankind would be spiritually and intellectually crippled. It frequently happens that artists are in some degree anti-social, or even worse because art tends to be an all-absorbing activity which closes the artist's eyes to common and distracting duties.

G.K. Chesterton, on the other hand, does not think that there is any 'doctor's dilemma' in the play. He argues that Shaw himself is doubtful about the raison d'etre of this particular problem. Is it an exasperating problem, after all? An artist of vast power and promise, who is also immoral, has a chance of life if specially treated for a special disease. The question of treating him with a special disregard because he is ethically anti-social is irrelevant. In affairs of life and death, one should never think of the distinctions like clever man and bad man. So the problem, if at all it is a problem, appears an artificial one.

To understand the exigency of the problem, the reader has to appraise one of the principal characters of the play—Sir Colenso Ridgeon. He has to give 'a life-and-death' answer in a critical situation in which he has either to cure the dull and inconspicuous good man Blenkinsop or save the painter-genius but unscrupulous Louis Dubedat. Sir Patrick Cullen, who represents humanity's fundamental moral sense, suggests to Dr. Ridgeon that he should cure both Louis Dubedat and Blenkinsop so that Dr. Ridgeon might not be accused of partial judgment. But the problem arises out of the typical predilections of Ridgeon's temperament. First, he is preoccupied by the notion of curing a chosen patient. Secondly, he is ardently susceptible to the charms of women. The problem is actually discussed by Dr. Ridgeon; Sir Patrick offers from the moral and humanitarian standpoint a practical solution. He tacitly denies the possibility of the fusion between essential goodness and great artistic powers in one person. The world is not going to be made so simple. Ultimately, Ridgeon saves Blenkinsop and allows Dubedat to die not because he chooses the good man in preference to the immoral genius but because he has fallen in love with Louis Dubedat's wife Jennifer. He has, thus, made the issue more complex.

Though Shaw has envisaged one of life's paradoxes viz. 'though art is ennobling, the artist may be ignoble,' he does not seem to have convincingly presented this aspect of the problem. Shaw has not portrayed Dubedat as a genius. A.C. Ward rightly remarks, "Dubedat is one of Shaw's major failures." The psychological delineation of Dubedat's character is too crude to be convincing. The incidents intended to show him up have been presented artificially. Dubedat appears to be a dismal relic of the decadent 'art for art's sake' movement. His sketching heads on the back of the menu cards (Act II) suggests that he was at best a thoroughgoing artificial aesthetic. Shaw has not convincingly presented the force of his imagination. Dubedat is at best a man with a genuine gift of drawing. His last picture is painted on his wife's mind not a truthful likeness but one most flattering to his vanity. On other occasions, he is clever but slight and small.

Thus by saving Blenkinsop and leaving Dubedat, Dr. Ridgeon does not seem to have preferred a moral man to an immoral artist. Even Shaw appears to be ambivalent regarding his approval of a man of goodness against a scoundrel with creative powers. Surprisingly, the ambiguity of Ridgeon's motive in sacrificing Dubedat and saving 'The Worthy' Blenkinsop raises the following questions:

(i) Did he do so because he thought with Sir Patrick that good man was more important than a painter of good pictures?
(ii) Was he ardently infatuated by Jennifer Dubedat?
(iii) Did he want to save her from the shock of finding her husband a poor creature whom she supposed to be the King of Men?

MacCarthy believes that probably all the three motives actuated Dr. Ridgeon.

The artificial problem of *The Doctor's Dilemma* has not been succinctly presented through the texture of the play. The major characters are shadowy and lack poignancy and vitality. Is it because Shaw's play is an after-thought, the first thoughts being expounded in the *Preface*? Is the ambivalent nature of the problem attributed to the enigmatic nature of human predicament itself? Shaw's play adumbrates not only the absurdity of the solution to a problem but that of the problem itself.

Naturalism and Beyond: The Poetic Element in John Galsworthy's Plays

B.N. KULKARNI

As a painter of the physical universe and of the soul, John Galsworthy is a poet.

Cazamian

John Glasworthy (1867-1933), a Nobel Prize winner, has left an indelible mark on both the forms of literature—the novel and the drama. The novel mattered to D.H. Lawrence, who called it 'one bright book of life.' His dramatic compositions were, however, less impressive. G.B. Shaw claimed that, like Shakespeare, he was a born dramatist, though, according to Raymond Williams, 'the emotional inadequacy of his plays denies him major status.'[1] Against this background, Galsworthy's successful handling of both the major forms stands out as a rare literary achievement.

For a decade he drew large audiences to theatres. He continued to flourish as a playwright despite the fact that the general literary climate was not favourable to him. He was, undoubtedly, a champion of the 'underdog' and an advocate of the theatre of dissent. He did not however, have (so the argument goes) the first-hand experience of what it feels like to be born poor and underprivileged, due to his 'elitist' status. Since poverty makes a difference of kind and not merely of degree, only those who are 'born working class' can write with authenticity about their way of life—their joys and sorrows, their tears and laughter—yes, said Lawrence, there were moments of uninhibited laughter in their lives, though the higher classes might be surprised at this news. Obviously, the argument has a touch of snobbery of a kind. It is not tenable, it never was.

Galsworthy, gifted with imaginative sympathy, presented with a naturalistic technique, a credible picture of the life of the classes into which he was not born. At a time when the strident tattoo of Shaw's swift-sailing ship nearly drowned all other voices, Galsworthy continued to speak with a level tone.

Modernism was another aggressive trend he had to reckon with. Virginia Woolf, for instance, dismissed the naturalistic representations of reality as superficial. Concerned with revealing 'the flickerings of that innermost flame which flashes its messages through the brain,'[2] she expressed dissatisfaction with the over-materiality of Galsworthy and his likes. They failed, according to her, to make audible the mind's inaudible conversations and wasted their time and energy in describing trivial external details. It would have been artistic to direct the torchlight to the rich inner self. Fully aware of the literary cross-currents, Galsworthy chose to follow his own vision and demonstrated, through a series of plays and novels, that an espousal of social causes need not, necessarily, run counter to the demands of art. A naturalistic play can be artistic too.

An exponent of naturalism, he often adopts an objective photographic technique to depict everyday conflicts in contemporary society. He portrays man as a victim of the social and economic forces beyond his control and understanding. In some of his plays, there are accurate descriptions of the dwelling places of the poor. Maeterlinck could be right when he remarked that one cannot look into the soul as one can, into a room. G.S. Fraser thinks that Galsworthy intended 'to present an example and state a case.'[3] This is far from true. Galsworthy's plays are not mechanical demonstrations of a formula. They are informed with genuine human warmth for the helpless, suffering human beings. He is not, therefore, content with describing a dwelling place only. He does try to look into the soul.

His plays fall broadly into two categories. *The Silver Box* (1906), *Strife* (1909) and *Justice* (1910) deal with social and economic problems. Social injustice, disparity between the rich and the poor, conflicting interests of capital and labour, and separate confinement of the prisoners—these issues figure prominently in these plays, which were highly successful on the stage. The playwright employs all the resources at his command—both verbal and non-verbal—to make the dramatic presentation effective.

The second group comprises plays like *Joy* (1907), *A Little Dream* (1911) and *A Bit o' Love* (1915). They are concerned with exploring relationships of the individuals among themselves against the background of nature. Mountains, open spaces and rivers have something Wordsworthian about them. The people involved do not have to contend with impersonal forces like the factories and the courts of law. Galsworthy the poet, is at his best, weaving magic with words. Imagination rather than logic, rhythm rather than argument hold the sway. He is almost romantic though he disliked the appellation. A romantic artist, according to him, is a person whose temperamental purpose is invention of tale or design with a view to delight himself and others.[4] The plays with poetic dimension reveal his versatility as a writer.

The Silver Box performed in the theatre of dissent, presents with naturalistic technique, a stark picture of social and legal injustice—or, rather, different kinds of justice, one for the underprivileged and other for the upper classes with power and pelf. Jack Barthwick, a Liberal M.P.'s son, and Jones, an underdog, commit a similar crime. Both are looked upon as a nuisance to the community. Jack is, however, let off while Jones is given a light sentence—one month with hard labour. On hearing the verdict, Jones feels outraged and blurts out:

> Call this justice? What about 'im? 'E got drunk!—'e took the purse but it's 'is money got 'im off—Justice!"
>
> (III, p. 47)[5]

The terse dialogues and quick exchanges heighten the dramatic quality of the court scenes. More effective is, however, the playwright's concern and sympathy for Mr. and Mrs. Jones, particularly the latter who suffers silently. The inexorable incompatibility between justice and what is just is ultimately traced to the class feelings and socio-economic determinism.

Strife is his most powerful play. It is classical in form and there is a strict observance of the unities. The action takes place on February 7th, between the hours of noon and six in the afternoon, close to the Trenartha Tin Plate Works, where the strike has been in progress throughout the winter.

Apparently, the play dramatizes the clash of interests between capital and labour. The company, with John Anthony as its founder Chairman is not willing to concede the demands of the workmen. The Union has withdrawn its support to the strike and now the workmen are led by Roberts, one from among themselves but 'a fanatical firebrand.' The company's losses are on the rise and so are the sufferings of the workers, starving or nearly so. Both the Directors and the workmen would like to see the end of the strike. John Anthony, a man of principles, is firm—'no surrender,' 'no compromise.' 'Masters are masters, men are men! Yield one demand and they will make it six. They are like Oliver Twist, asking for more!' (III, p. 151) Edgar, his son and one of the Directors, and Enid, his daughter, plead with their father to bring to an end the suffering and starvation of workmen's families. Harness, the union official, is equally sympathetic. He is in a conciliatory mood. He wants to have done with 'this old-fashioned tug-of-war business.' He says, "these people are men like yourselves, and want, what's good for them, just as you want what's good for you." (I, p. 108)

Roberts is much tougher. He is blunt, bitter and sarcastic. He minces no words. He says to the Chairman: 'Every man of us is well-nigh starving—ye needn't think that by waiting ye'll drive us to come in—we'll die first, the whole lot of us.' Roberts refuses to withdraw a single demand while Anthony turns down all their demands.

The deadlock continues. Enid's fervent appeal, 'Father! Do stop it for my sake,' falls on deaf ears. Edgar pleads that there is such a thing as mercy to which Anthony retorts: 'And Justice comes before it!' (III, p. 152)

As the play swiftly moves on, from the beginning, through the middle to the close, it becomes clear that it is not a conflict between capital and labour that forms the theme of the play. It is a head-on clash between Anthony and Roberts, both driven by their egoistic impulse. The directors and the workmen want compromise. The former threw over Anthony and the latter hooted out Roberts. Once the egoistic Chairman and the obstinate leader were out of the way, there was a settlement of the dispute, but not before an avoidable tragedy had struck: 'A woman dead; and two best men broken.' And ironically, both the Directors and the workmen accepted the very terms that were put to both sides before the situation had worsened! Tench comments: "All this—all this—and and what for?" (III, p. 156)

As in a classical Greek play, the action moves fast like a swift arrow towards the denouement. Everything 'clicks to' and not a scene is dispensable. There are no long speeches to mar the dramatic effect. Galsworthy's imaginative sympathy is at work through Edgar, Enid and Thomas. Robert's proud but innocent wife is the casualty of the head-on clash of the two dominant personalities.

Joseph Conrad was convinced that there would be "Such a shout (of praise) around *Strife* as this country has not heard for a hundred years or more."[6]

Galsworhty describes *Justice* as 'A Tragedy.' There is, apparently, very little 'heroic' about Falder who forges a cheque in order to elope with a married woman he loves. His true and uncompromising love for Ruth is both his strength and weakness. It reveals the spiritual dimension of his personality and at the same time it drives him to commit felony in a moment of temporary insanity. Here, in the words of Meredith, 'Passions spin the . . . plot.' No villain is around unless it is Destiny. Falder is not made of sterner stuff. All along, he has a feeling of being hunted. "The fact is, I seem to be struggling against a thing that's all around me. I can't explain it—it is as if I was in a net." (IV, p. 266) This is almost like a Kafka character articulating himself in a hesitant faltering manner. Though James thinks that Falder is a 'weak character and brought it all on himself.' Walter's comment is significant: "The doctrine of full responsibility doesn't quite hold in these days." (IV, p. 268)

James How, Falder's employer, was willing to take him back after he was released from prison, on condition that he should give up Ruth. He fiercely refused. Things, however, took a different turn when Falder was re-arrested for forging references. He reached the limit of his endurance and flung himself to death. Cokeson spoke the last words: "No one will touch him now. He's safe with Gentle Jesus!" (IV, p. 274) Falder, therefore, is beaten in his struggle with society.

But, through this play, Galsworthy made an important contribution to the cause of penal reform in England. There is a special pleading for treating the convicts humanely. Galsworthy remarked that the separate confinement had been the horror to nervous prisoners. The technique used in the 'cell' scene (III.iii, pp. 260-61) is simply unique. Falder is undergoing 'separate confinement.' The turbulence of his mind, his restlessness, suppressed violence—all these are conveyed through his movements in the cell. The 'verbal primacy' is replaced by gestures only. Not a word is spoken. The silences and pauses herald a new technique.

"After the initial bare, accurate and prosaic details of the set, there follows the restless ritual of the prisoner's movements, where the body tells of the mind's agony," and "after the cell-light is clicked on—we and the prisoner are thrown into a symbolism of light and noise."[7] Galsworthy has, thus, transcended the limits of naturalism.

Joy (1907) is altogether a different kind of play. The action takes place outdoors. "The time is morning and the scene, a level lawn, beyond which the river is running amongst fields. A huge old beech tree with a hollow that hides many things. The sky is clear and sunny." It is Colonel Hope's country house. The setting, the tone, the theme and the general atmosphere are anything but naturalistic in the technical sense of the term. It is the country and not the town. The sub-title is: 'a play on the letter I.' Each of the characters, with the exception of the old governess Miss Beech, is a slave to his or her ego. Pride blocks the vision of the things as they are. Each regards himself or herself as a special case. Thanks to the magic of love, the walls become less opaque in the end.

Joy is a sympathetic, almost a poetic study of the psychology of an adolescent girl, who, deprived of her father's affection, wants her mother, Molly Gwyn, all to herself. Possessive and jealous, she hates Maurice Lever, her mother's lover. The play has a romantic glow about it. Mrs. Hope, the Colonel's wife, is domineering but she has 'roses in her hands.' The issue of investing in the gold mines is hotly debated by the Colonel and his wife but it is not central to the play. Under the influence of the pleasant atmosphere, Mr. Lever presents the true facts about the gold mines

Company which he had recommended to the Colonel earlier. There are, therefore, no specific tensions resulting from ideological or social conflict. Joy is the central character. So, much consumed with jealousy, she keeps Dick Merton at an arm's distance, though he worships the very ground she treads on. The play ends with Joy being won over by Dick Merton through genuine love for her. Dick says: "But look here, Joy, this'll show you! If a person loves a person, they have to decide, haven't they? Well, then, you see, that's what mother's done." (III, p. 95) Thus, he helps Joy to understand her mother better. The dialogue continues:

Joy: Oh, Dick, you are so sweet and—and—funny.
DickI love you Joy. I'll love you all day and everyday—It's such a beautiful night—Look. But it is not so beautiful as you. (III, p. 96)

The playwright's comments follow: 'the waltz sounds louder' and 'she looks at him, and her face changes, suddenly she buries it against his shoulder. . . . They stand so just a moment in the moonlight, then turning to the river move slowly out of sight.' (III, p. 96)

It is only when Joy falls in love that she begins to understand her mother—why she was so passionately attached to Mr. Lever. Miss Beech has the words of wisdom for all concerned: "They must go their own ways, poor things! she can't put herself in the child's place and the child can't put herself in Molly's—A woman and a girl—there's the tree of life between them" and further, "There's suffering enough, without adding to it our trumpery judgements!" (III, p. 97)

The young lovers, however, seem to have the last word:

Joy: [In a whisper] Dick, is love always like this!
Dick[Putting his arms round her, with conviction] *It's never been like this before—It's you and me!* [He kisses her on the lips]

Joy, with its sunny sky and moonlit night, its roses and breezes and love is worlds apart from the photographic naturalism of *The Silver Box*. To some the play is 'flimsy.' To others, it is true to life. "Mr. Galsworthy has helped to lay in *Joy* one of the foundation-stones of our future drama," says A.B. Walkley. The play affords a glimpse of the enlarged vision of human relationships, estranged by the ego but ultimately harmonised by love.

Like *Joy, The Little Dream* (1911) is remote from the worldly concerns and violent conflicts that figure in some of the other plays of Galsworthy. The playlet projects a fantasy of Seelchen, a mountain-girl who is fascinated by Lamond, a climber from a city. She keeps dreaming about the city and asks him several questions about the city life-style. Lamond, young and tanned, has climbed the lower peaks, the Cow Horn and the Wine Horn. Now he has come 'to go up the Great Horn at sunrise.' He is not deterred by Seelchen's warning: 'But he—the Great Horn, is so dangerous—it is perhaps death.' 'One must take one's chance,' he replies. He needs a guide and would approach Felsman, her local friend. The girl, however, aching for the moon, would like to see the big world of the towns and the cities. The play is made up of a series of dreams in which Seelchen converses with the mountain peaks, with Lamond and Felsman. Each of them offers her something but she soon gets tired of what is offered and moves on to something different. Perhaps, The Great Horn is the final stop.

The Cow Horn says to her: 'Little soul, Hold to me! Love me! Live with me under the stars.' (ii, p. 207) The Cow Horn speaks for Felsman and the mountains. But the Wine Horn tempts her, speaking in a young man's voice, "I am the town—the will-o'-the wisp that dances through the streets—the life of men in crowds is mine—of lamp lights in the streets at dawn." (ii, p. 207)

And so, it goes on—both the country and the city continue to entice her. The former, the Cow Horn, assured her certainty, peace and stillness and one love; the latter, the Wine Horn, promises her chance, change, voice and many loves. Seelchen, unable to choose either, would like to have both—"both, both will love." The Great Horn, however, suggests that these are the two sides of human life: "And both thou shalt love little soul! Thou shalt lie on the hills with silence; and dance in the cities with knowledge. Both shall possess thee!" (ii, p. 208)

In the next sequence, she dreams of being in the town with Lamond who waxes poetic. "To love is to live. . . . Seeking for wonder. . . . When a feather flies, is it not loving the wind, the unknown? come to my town!" (iii, pp. 210-11) But, soon she gets fed up with the town life: "The windy hours through darkness fly. Hear them, little heart? New loves are born, and old loves die, And kissing lips must part." (iii, p. 211)

Seelchen, the little soul is pale, as if wan with living. Leaving the love-lorn Lamond, she returns to the mountain side, to the Cow Horn, and to her country admirer, Felsman. She tells him she has known change and is no longer a timid maid. Felsman notices that she has undergone a change for the worse. Her eyes are hollow and she is white-faced. He offers her "the sun, the air, the silence," and "the flowers shall dance to thee." (iv, p. 214) But, this cannot hold her. She says, "I go ever onward." In the penultimate scene, the Great Horn philosophizes:

> Thou traveller to the tideless Sea,
> Where light and dark and change and peace,
> Are one—come, little soul, to Mystery! (v, p. 216)

Perhaps, this is the voice of harmony of something beyond the country and the town—beyond certainty and change. The Great Horn is the Higher Presence that absorbs little things and little souls (like those of Seelchen). Thus, Galsworthy has tried to explore the poetic dimension of life. He said, "The deeper symbolism of *The Little Dream* is so personal to me so intimate that I rather despair of making it clear in prose."[9]

R.H. Coats thinks that in its appeal to *imaginative sympathy* lies the quintessential flavour of a Galsworthy play.[10] Mentioning a symbolic, meditative speech of the Great Horn, Coats remarks, with some surprise, "Yet there are some who think that Galsworthy is not a poet." (212)

In conclusion, it may be stated that this brief account of a great playwright's achievements is an attempt to substantiate the view that it is the poetic element that has enriched his plays, raising them to a high, artistic level.

NOTES

1. Raymond Williams, *Drama from Ibsen to Brecht* (England: Penguin, 1967), pp. 169-70.
2. Virginia Woolf, *The Common Reader* (England: Penguin, 1938), p. 150.
3. G.S. Fraser, *The Modern Writer and This World* (England: Penguin, 1964), p. 197.
4. A.D. Choudhari, *Galsworthy's Plays* (Bombay: Orient Longmans, 1961), p. 8.
5. John Galsworthy, *The Plays of John Galsworthy* (London: Duckworth, 1935)
6. Choudhari, p. 66.
7. G.L. Evans, *The Language of Modern Drama* (London: J.M. Dent, 1977), pp. 72-73.
8. Choudhari, p. 108.
9. Choudhari, p. 120
10. R.H. Coats, *John Galsworthy as a Dramatic Artist* (London: Duckworth, 1926), p. 198.

The Theatre of the Absurd

PRASHANT K. SINHA

Much before Martin Esslin coined the term the "Theatre of the Absurd," playwrights had shown in their plays, individual elements which later crystallized as distinctive features of this wave in theatre. As Jan Kott mentions in his seminal study of Shakespeare, *Shakespeare, Our Contemporary*, plays like *Hamlet* and *King Lear* project an essentially meaningless universe and in Peter Brook's productions, based mainly on Kott's thesis, one can discern traits of the Absurd. When Hamlet cries out that "The time is out of joint" or Gloucester speaks in anguish,

> As Flies to
> Wanton boys, are we to the gods
> They kill us for their sport

we are made aware of the lack of a moral scheme and ultimate meaning in the world. Similarly Hamlet's celebrated soliloquy, "To be or not to be" powerfully highlights existential choice that he has to make.

The first notable predecessor of the Absurd in our own epoch was Chekhov. His characters cannot understand the mystery of universe and wonder why they are living at all. *The Three Sisters* ends with the sisters huddled together at the news of Baron Tuzenbach's death which effectively terminates the possibility of Irina, the youngest getting married and wondering if one day the mystery of the universe would be revealed to them. Till then they have to go on living without knowing why. Chekhov's characters drift and lose the capacity to act. In *The Sea Gull*, Trepleff can make nothing out of his life. Andrey in *The Three Sisters*, Vanya in *Uncle Vanya* and Gayev in *The Cherry Orchard* completely fail to come to grips with the reality confronting them and do something to control the situation and act decisively.

The characters of Chekhov are lonely and isolated and they fail to communicate with each other. The multiple interlocking triangles in *The Sea Gull* involving Medvedev, Masha, Trepleff, Nina, Trigorin and Arkadina pertinently illustrate the inability of characters to communicate meaningfully. The many deaf servants like Ferapont in *The Three Sisters* and Firs in *The Cherry Orchard* demonstrate the failure of interpersonal communication. Often characters indulge in their own monologues and talk at cross purposes about different topics. Thus Chekhov demolishes the traditional concept of dialogue in drama. Moreover, in his plays, silence often conveys more than speech. This emphasis on communication through silence and sound effects was derived by Chekhov from the Belgian-French Symbolist playwright Maeterlinck in whose works like *The Intruder*, a lot more is transmitted through the non-human/non-verbal sounds than through the dialogues. This was as in *The Ghost Sonata* by Maeterlinck's admirer Strindberg in which the colonel and his wife, Mummy, never talk to each other because they have nothing to hide from each other.[1]

Maeterlinck's impressionism was also parallelled in Chekhov's attempt to evolve an atmosphere through the careful creation of the scene, the season, the time of the day and the various audio effects. The fire siren in *The Three Sisters* or the sound of the breaking string in *The Cherry Orchard* create the atmosphere which highlights the predicament of several characters facing a similar fate. The situation becomes central to the plays as the plot is gradually banished and we move towards the drama of indirect action leading to the drama of inaction.

The expressionists and the surrealists with their subjective presentation of reality and the emphasis on dreams, reveries and hallucinations coupled with fantastic and bizarre events prepared the way for the strange world of the Absurdists as a projection of the subconscious perception of reality. The old man crowing like a rooster and the Mummy behaving like a parrot in *The Ghost Sonata* distinctly anticipate the weird world of Ionesco's *Rhinoceros* and *Amédée*.

The other major predecessor in theatre was Pirandello who repeatedly dramatized the themes of illusion and reality, showing in plays like *Six Characters in Search of an Author* and *Henry IV* that we cannot clearly differentiate one from the other, partly because words, the vehicles of differentiation, are not exact. His characters also have fluid or multiple identities e.g. Mrs. Ponza, the mysterious wife in *Right You Are*. Many of these characters also play roles and these roles often merge into the self, the mask into the face as with the unnamed Henry IV. The role-playing sometimes becomes more formal and the play then crystallizes around a play within the play as in *Six Characters in Search of an Author*.

The vision of an Absurd meaningless universe had also emerged prominently in European fiction in the works of Kafka. The entire process of the arrest, prosecution and punishment of Joseph K. in *The Trial* suggests as irrational and absurd a world as the inexplicable experience of the confused Land Surveyor in *The Castle* who can never reach the castle.

However, the most immediate impetus came from the philosophical and literary writings of Sartre and "Atheistic Existentialists" as distinguished from the Christian Existentialists like Kierkegaard, Marcel and Jaspers. In the Sartrean vision, embodied in many of his works, but most systematically and lucidly in *Existentialism and Humanism*, an essentially godless—as in Nietzsche who had announced the death of god—and meaningless, irrational universe without any order, purpose and goal is postulated. Naturally there are no absolute values in such a world, and human existence is not informed by any benign cause in a universe in which logic cannot explain anything. A man is an alien from nature, like M. Roquentin in Sartre's *Nausea*, and he is isolated from other men. As Sartre shows in his play *No Exit*, "Hell is other people" and conflict is the only basis of human relationships. At the same time, he also has a positive side in his emphasis on the need for every individual to create his own set of values. When making a moral choice, a person chooses for all humanity and asks himself what if everyone acted that way. He should invest his life with meaning and act in order to affirm his way of life as Orestes does in *The Flies*. Since man is not predetermined, but "condemned to be free," he can shape the course of his life and he must go through a phase of anguish and despair when making his momentous choices which place onerous responsibilities for mankind on him. The Theatre of the Absurd, however, ignores the more positive side of Sartre's Existential position.

Camus, whose philosophy of the Absurd perhaps gave this nomenclature to the movement, expounded his concept of the human predicament in *The Myth of Sisyphus*. Just as Sisyphus keeps on raising the stone up the hill which constantly rolls down, all the efforts of man end in vain without achieving anything. Nonetheless, "one must imagine Sisyphus happy." Similarly a human being must confront the absurdity of a universe in which the "fact of one's eventual death" negates everything. Although the mind's need for "unity" and the "chaos of the world the mind experiences" do not correspond with each other, the rage for order must not be snuffed out by the awareness of death. Even the "disproportionate" gap between the appearance and reality of things makes one aware of cosmic absurdity. As Camus mentions, feeling of absurdity can strike one on account of any of the following: an awareness of time passing, of time as a destructive force; a consciousness of the mechanical nature of our lives; a feeling of being an alien in the universe; a sense of isolation from other human beings. Camus suggests that in the teeth of this awareness, one can act in one of these three ways: by committing suicide, obliterate this tormenting awareness of absurdity; ignore the absurd nature of existence by mentally escaping from it in a manner reminiscent of Kierkegaard's "leap of faith"; one can face the absurd and still create meaning and purpose out of it. Camus rejects physical suicide and the Kierkegaardian "leap of faith" which he dubs mental suicide. However, this positive emphasis in the Camusian philosophy is missing from the absurd plays.

Sartre and Camus expounded their visions in the conventional format by simply arguing within the traditional framework of a play. The playwrights of the Theatre of Absurd, on the contrary, created a new form which adequately embodied their different outlook on the world. To an extent, it combined this world view with the mode of Surrealism. As Block and Shedd record in their introduction to *The Bald Soprano*, Ionesco agreed that there is the surreal in his plays, but he claimed that he was more lucid in his organisation of dreams and other subconscious experiences. Like them, he views art as "the exteriorization of a psychic dynamics."[2] In fact J.L. Styan called it "a short lived eruption of surrealistic drama which came to be known as 'theatre of the absurd.'"[3] The "movement" converged around a group of expatriate writers settled in France after the Second World War: Eugene Ionesco, Samuel Beckett and Arthur Adamoff, each one of them writing mainly in French. Their major Continental followers were Gunther Grass and Fernando Arrabal.

Jean Genet, who provided a link with Pirandello, through his emphasis on the motif of role-playing, the format of the play within the play and the theme of overlapping natures of art and life, appearance and reality, mask and face and the fluid nature of human identity, shares a lot in common with the Theatre of the Absurd in plays like *The Maids* and *The Balcony*. What are the real names of the Bishop, the Judge and the General? Do they have separate identities? How does the "poisoning" of the sister in the "rehearsal" (i.e. the "poisoning" of the Madame) become the real act? The impossibility of providing definitive answers to these questions links Genet clearly with the Absurdists. But as Robert Brustein points out in The Theatre of Revolt, his drama also reveals many attributes of the "Theatre of Cruelty" inspired by Antonin Artaud.[4]

In their major works, the absurdists postulated a meaningless, purposeless universe which defies any attempt at a rational explanation. In fact, most of the events that take place cannot be explained by logic. How is it that men are converted into rhinoceros? What makes a dead corpse grow constantly? Why should Nag and Nell be kept confined in dustbins?[5] These are questions which cannot be answered in a rational way. The plays proceed even further to suggest that logic is at fault as a tool of epistemology. Thus in Ionesco's *The Bald Soprano,* the call bell rings thrice and when the hosts open the door, they find nobody there. So they—Mr. and Mrs. Smith—have a detailed argument on the proposition that when the doorbell rings, it means that there is no one there. As Block and Shedd mention in their "Introduction" to the play, the work is replete with "incongruous analogies, arbitrary associations, forced and ridiculous inferences, and gross distortions of the familiar and commonplace." (18)

In these plays, people do not behave in a rational or logical way. In *Waiting for Godot*, Pozzo walks with a rope tied round the neck of Lucky as if he is an animal, and the latter, in spite of his brutal treatment, weeps when Pozzo offers to leave him. Mr. and Mrs. Martin of *The Bald Soprano* do not recognize each other till after a tortuous process, they realize that they are husband and wife.

In fact, the Absurd playwrights neither fill in the backgrounds of characters nor explain their motivations. Why are Vladimir and Estragon waiting for Godot? What is the background of these two tramps? Why should the family in Ionesco's *Jaques. or the Submission* insist that every member like the potatoes in their jackets? What motivations can a woman like Winnie have (in Beckett's *Happy Days*) for sitting in a mound of sand and what is her background?

Several major characters do not even have a fixed sense of identity. In Act I of *Waiting for Godot*, Pozzo can see and Lucky can speak, but in Act II, Pozzo is blind and Lucky is dumb. The boy who comes in Act I, comes again in Act II but Estragon does not recognize him and he himself denies having come earlier as Godot's messenger. The whole personality of Krapp (in *Krapp's Last Tape*) disintegrates as he reminisces over the past. At the end of *The Bald Soprano*, Mr. and Mrs. Martin replace Mr. and Mrs. Smith. The characters also change their identities at least temporarily when they play roles. The many games that Vladimir and Estragon play also involve their assumption of different roles. They also lead to the theme of appearance and reality and the gap between them.

On the other hand the failure of the Boy and Estragon to corroborate the events associated with the former's last visit point to the unreliability of human memory. Now, memory as a construct of Time reflects the concern of the Absurd Theatre with the problems of Time—a la Camus. In a different manner, Ionesco has referred to the problem of the undependability of objective time by showing that the clock of Mr. and Mrs. Smith never strikes the right note.

Not only do the characters in these plays have no local habitations, but the settings themselves are carefully abstracted in such a way that the action cannot be located in space or time. If Vladimir is Russian, Estragon French, Pozzo Italian and Lucky English, in which country is *Godot* set and in which period? The invariably small number of characters in these plays further prevents the creation of social details and a crowded human canvas. The absurd play presents the unchanging human situation and not the specific problems of a particular community which can be solved by reforming the society or its institutions.

These characters in the Absurd plays are not only put in some no man's land, but within the groups themselves, they are also isolated from each other and unable to communicate with each other. They have nothing to communicate and language fails as a medium of communication. As David Galloway says, "The general devaluation of the language in the absurd art springs from two sources: a distrust of the outmoded 'realities' embodied in it, and a tragic sense of the failure of communication in modern culture."[6] Thus in Beckett's *Act without Words*, there are no speeches at all—only physical movements. *EhJoe* has no dialogue and the play is like a mime. In fact the theatre of the Absurd was inspired by pantomimes and puppet shows. To take up Ionesco, at the beginning of *The Bald Soprano*, Mrs. Smith's repeated attempts to carry on a conversation meet with total silence from Mr. Smith who is engaged in his newspaper. At the end of the play, the breakdown of language is so complete that characters mechanically and in a ritualistic manner repeat the letters of the alphabet or say "Krishnamurthy, Krishnamurthy" or "Such cascades of cacas." The voices that the protagonist of Beckett's *That Time* hears have no links whatsoever with each other and one can "understand" the play only if one reads all the speeches of A in succession and then those of B in sequence and finally those of C continuously. Quite appropriately the plays of the Absurd variety have short sentences and brief curt speeches, indicating lack of continuity which is also shown by the many coordinate clauses. Cliches abound suggesting that language has lost its freshness and words their meaning. As Styan says "The dialogue is no more than a series of inconsequential cliches which reduce those who speak them to talking machines." (II, 126) There is also a general lack of harmony between words and actions. At the end of each act of *Waiting for Godot* both Estragon and Vladimir say that they should go and immediately, the stage direction reads "*They do not move.*"[7]

These plays do not have plots. A plot implies a logical sequence of cause and effect which parallels the conception of an orderly universe, but in the Absurd plays there is no logical construction or the rational linking of idea with idea. So these plays lack plot and more than that events. As Martin Esslin writes in *The Theatre of the Absurd* an Absurd play has a situation rather than a story. Less and less happens in these plays as in Beckett's works like *Happy Days* or *Endgame.* We often end where we started as in *Waiting for Godot.* What is important is the creation of a mood, an atmosphere that informs the entire play. The lack of action reflects the quintessentially dull and monotonous nature of our lives, also reinforced in some plays by dull and boring dialogues. The strong element of repetition in the plays further emphasizes it. Life itself is seen as repetitive like Sisyphus rolling the rock up the hill. Thus the two acts of *Waiting for Godot* are almost identical—only the tree has four or five leaves in the Second Act. In each act, Vladimir and Estragon are visited by Lucky and Pozzo and a boy comes to inform them that Godot will not come. Both the acts end with the decision of Vladimir and Estragon to move without any of them actually doing so.

Although Beckett translated his plays himself into English and even wrote occasionally in English, he is essentially in the Continental rather than the English tradition. Pinter and Stoppard represent the highest peaks of the British Absurd plays, and an analysis of their works like *The Birthday Party, The Caretaker, The Dumb Waiter, The Home Coming* and *Rosencrantz and Guildenstern are Dead* can bring out the precise way in which these two masters gave the movement in the 1950s and 60s a distinctively native hue. Although John Whiting's *Conditions of Agreement* had in its dialogues and the strange behaviour of drifting characters, shown some evidence of the Absurd, the first genuine experiment in the genre was Pinter's *The Birthday Party.*

Pinter revealed a remarkable element of the Absurd in his presentation of the characters. Motivations and backgrounds are singularly mysterious in play after play. Why is Stanley in *The Birthday Party* hiding in his resort and from which organization? How is it that he so easily falls a prey to the machinations of Goldberg and McCann? By what twist in the plot is one killer asked to kill the other in *The Dumb Waiter*? Even in *The Homecoming* which Martin Esslin has tried to explain at the "realistic" level in his book,[8] it is obvious that the speed with which Ruth allows Joey to jump into bed with her and Lenny to convert her into a prostitute and the ready acquiescence of her husband, Teddy—in fact his willingness to act as her promoter—are implausible enough to fit into the pattern of the Absurd plays. Their irrational behaviours also point to a larger irrationality in the world around them which cannot be explained in logical terms and which, to an extent, shows the limitations of logic as a mode of perception. As Richard Schechner states, Pinter's heroes like Kafka's are vague about what is going to happen.[9] At the same time, as Alrene Sykes points out, "Pinter's plays suggest that life is uncertain, but not necessarily that it is also inevitably devoid of purpose, senseless in the way that Beckett, Ionesco, Arrabal, Vian, Adamoff and Pinget have implied."[10]

Pinter has also tried frequently to take up the motif of role playing. Sarah and Richard, the wife and the husband, repeatedly playing the whore and the gallant constitute the core of the action of *The Lover*. Lenny constantly plays a role when dealing with Ruth. Meg plays the role of the Belle at Stanley's birthday party.

Sometimes the characters also reveal fluid identities e.g when Edward, the husband, is asked to hold the matchstick and the match-seller replaces the husband in *A Slight Ache*. The abrupt conversion of Ruth, a housewife into a prostitute, also suggests her lack of a solid, concrete identity. Davies tells people that his name is Jenkins.

These characters, however, unlike those of Beckett, do not operate in some no man's land. Plays like *The Birthday Party, The Caretaker, The Dumb Waiter, The Homecoming*, and *Old Times* have distinct "local habitations," and in many of them social details are recreated at some length even though the number of characters in Pinter's drama invariably remains small.

The plays of Pinter also do not eschew plot. There are plots even in those plays which like *The Dumb Waiter* show mechanically repetitive actions such as Gus repeatedly untying his shoe laces, taking a match box and a cigarette box out, and tying them, Ben's eyes meeting him each time Gus does so and coming back to the newspaper. Although some plays like *The Caretaker, Lovers* and *Old Times* have scanty plots, Pinter, in general, creates suspense in his drama as he aims at comedies of menace—explained partly by the fact of his growing up as a Jewish boy in London during the Second World War when it was constantly threatened by the German Air Force. The tremendous excitement about what may happen to Stanley or to Ruth indicates the presence of a plot so uncharacteristic of a play by Beckett.

However, in the presentation of isolation of characters and their failure to communicate with each other, Pinter reveals distinctive features of the Absurd. Although Stanley often interacts with Meg, who flirts with him in a maternal way, he cannot communicate to her the motives or fears and premonitions that become the driving forces of his personality. Teddy, the professor of philosophy, cannot convey his abstract conceptions to his worldly family. Aston and Davies both need company and they fail to establish the proper relationship with each other in *The Caretaker*. Even when they first meet, they refuse to take any interest in each other's topics. Davies insists on talking about the monk in the monastery and on asking how many blacks are around while Aston concentrates on the shoes that he has to give to Davies. As Styan mentions, in *Landscape* and *Silence*, Pinter "has inclined towards Beckettian monologue." (II, 134)

Pinter shows the essentially dull and mechanical nature of language as a mode of communication. As Ronald Hayman points out, Pinter demonstrates the irrationality of everyday conversation, "its bad syntax, tautologies, pleonasms, repetitions, non-sequiturs and self-contradictions."[11] One can see this repetition in Davies' talk about his wife's slovenliness: "The pan for vegetables, it was the vegetable pan."

In his plays, characters tend to speak in short sentences—single clause sentence—or in short clauses. The speeches are brief. Sometimes the speakers contradict themselves to show the essential illogicality of what they are saying—in a larger sense of language itself. An example is the interrogation of Stanley by Goldberg and

McCann. Thus when Goldberg and McCann ask Stanley in the same breath why he killed his wife and why he never married, they become utterly illogical. The following questions that they ask are again not expected to be answered in a sensible, meaningful way:

Goldberg:	Who watered the wicket in Melbourne?
McCann:	What about the blessed Oliver Plunkett?
Goldberg:	Speak up Webber why did the chicken cross the road?
Stanley:	He wanted to—He wanted to—He wanted to.
McCann:	He doesn't know.
Goldberg:	Why did the chicken cross the road?
Stanley:	He wanted to
McCann:	He doesn't know. He does not know. Which came first?
Goldberg:	Which came first?
McCann:	Chicken? Egg? Which came first?
Goldberg and McCann:	Which came first? Which came first? Which came first?[12]

The above speech also provides a fine example of the typical short clipped sentences and clauses of the dialogue of Pinter. The speeches of the interrogators moreover contain jargons. Andrew Kennedy also refers appropriately to "Goldberg's cliche patter" in the same breath as "Mick's finance and interior-decorator terms" and "the academic jargon of Teddy." (167) Schechner provides a useful comment on Pinter's dialogues of short clipped sentences: "Both Pinter and Hemingway use stichomythia based on trivial ideas which suggest sinister happenings."[13]

Pinter like the typical Absurdists, Beckett and Ionesco, loves to play with language. Kennedy refers to "the variations rung on 'going the whole hog' in *The Homecoming* until Joey concludes that 'now and again . . . you can be happy . . . without going any hog at all.'" (167, fn.6) This relates to Jean Vannier's notion of the new drama as "a *theatre of language* where man's words are held up to us as a spectacle."[14]

These plays like the Continental Absurd plays show that often silences can convey more than words. Perhaps during his work for Sir Donald Wolfit's classical repertory company, Pinter acquired a taste for "long silences and long gestures." As he said when speaking of his script for the film *Accident in Sight and Sound* (Autumn 1966), "and it is this mystery which fascinates me. What happens between words, what happens when no words are spoken."[15] Some of the most powerful moments in Pinter are moments of silence. Thus in *Homecoming*, when Ruth confronts Lenny for the first time, they try to pour water down each other's throat while nothing is spoken. The fact that Ruth succeeds in doing so while Lenny fails, indicates her superiority in this trial of strength. The play ends with Max grovelling at Ruth's feet, Sam in a collapsed state on the floor and the other characters standing or sitting silent as the curtain comes down almost on a tableau. As John Russell Brown says, "during the final moments," a Pinter play "becomes a silent tableau."[16] Near the end of *The Dumb Waiter*, Gus and Wes face each other and speak nothing. *The Caretaker* ends with totally silent responses of Mick and Aston to Davies's pleading to them to let him remain there.

In a play like *Old Times,* Pinter takes up a major concern of the Absurdists: the unreliability of human memory. As Kate, Anna and Deeley try to remember the past, it becomes obvious that "recollections can be misleading" and therefore the truth of the past is impossible to arrive at. As Anna says, "there are some things one remembers even though they may never have happened. There are things I remember which may never have happened, but as I recall them so they take place."[17] This vagueness of time and memory distinctly echoes Beckett's *Waiting for Godot*.

Tom Stoppard has said of himself that he is distinguished by "an absolute lack of certainty about almost anything" and that he writes plays because "dialogue is the most respectable way of contradicting myself." His best known work *Rosencrantz and Guildenstern Are Dead* reveals both these features. At the very outset of the play as the protagonists are tossing the coins, Rosencrantz counts "Heads" eighty-five times. As the number rises higher to ninety two, it becomes obvious that in their world, the law of probability does not work at all. Like Vladimir and Estragon, with whom they are often compared, they do not know why they have to wait here. They are not quite sure why the King wants them. Later in the play, they cannot see a cosmic justification for their impending deaths. According to Benedict Nightingale, their deaths may indicate "the blind mechanical drift of a meaningless universe."[18] The play also marks the limits of logic in trying to explain the world leading to an awareness of the inadequacy of logic as a tool of epistemology. In the other major Stoppard play, *Jumpers*, all the abstract reasonings of George Moore, Professor of Moral Philosophy end in "agonized inconclusiveness" or "flustered irrelevance."

Language, the medium of this reasoning is itself shown to be illogical and arbitrary. Rosencrantz and Guidenstern play "Wittgenstein word-games" including one that consists entirely of questions. One finds in the plays "unexpected verbal connections, word games, puns" etc. (408) A good example is the later play *Dirty Linen* in which the dialogue consists only of "foreign phrases in familiar English use" interspersed with "bloody awkward" and "Pardon my French." Tom Stoppard plays with language to reveal its innate lack of logic.

The motif of playing is however dominantly manifested in the device of the play-within-the-play and the act of role-playing in *Rosencrantz and Guildenstern Are Dead.* Naturally, a "modernized version" of *Hamlet* is expected to be built around a central play-within-the-play. Here, however, the players overshadow many scenes and the two principal characters themselves play many roles. Thus they play at finding out what is wrong with Hamlet. Guildenstern tells Rosencrantz: "What we are attempting is a hypothesis in which I answer for *him* while you ask me questions."[19] Then Guildenstern plays Hamlet as Rosencrantz interrogates him. In the second act, they themselves are played by the players, "*Under their cloaks, the two* SPIES *are wearing coats identical to those worn by* ROS and GUIL, *whose coats are now covered by their cloaks.*" (62) In the third act, Rosencrantz becomes the King of England as they rehearse their future meeting with him. In the process, they "open" the letter. Later when Guildenstern plays the King, they open the letter which says that both of them be "put to sudden death." As the actors surround them, Guildenstern thrusts the dagger into the throat of the player who "dies."

These characters change their identities not only when playing roles but also elsewhere and in other situations. When the player and his troupe enter for the first time, Rosencrantz calls himself Guildenstern and calls Guildenstern Rosencrantz. As Claudius welcomes them he says "welcome dear Rosencrantz" and raises a hand at Guildenstern. Then he utters "and Guildenstern" raising a hand at Rosencrantz. This confusion of identities raises the possibility that everything is an illusion, that reality cannot be isolated from the illusion.

Unlike the play by Shakespeare which is steeped in the Renaissance culture and which has a distinct local habitation, our play begins with "*Two* ELIZABETHANS *passing the time in a place without any visible character.*" In fact the setting distinctly recalls the no man's land in which Vladimir and Estragon are waiting. At the same time, the large cast in the play, like that in *Jumpers* sets up a tension with the "abstracted" setting by filling in some of the social details. Above all, the play does not eschew plot. After all, things happen not only to the Prince of Denmark and the principal characters but also to the "attendant lords," Rosencrantz and Guildenstern.

Thus there are certain seminal differences between the attitudes of Beckett on one hand and Pinter and Stoppard on the other—differences which have become more pronounced with their development in time. Beckett moves towards an aesthetics of silence, Pinter and Stoppard continue to relish the use of language, to use language as a weapon and to play with language respectively. Both Pinter and Stoppard are firmly grounded in the contemporary social reality. Stoppard even engages the problems specific to his time in later plays like *Every Good Boy Deserves Favour, Professional Foul*, and *Cahoot's Macbeth*. Above all, the plays of both can be explained at the literal level as Martin Esslin has done in *The Peopled Wound: The Plays of Harold Pinter*. In contrast, Beckett and Ionesco almost invariably thwart any attempt at literal interpretation.

NOTES

1. Earlier in the play, Hummel, the Old Man, says silence cannot hide

one's thoughts which is more than what one can say for speech.

2. "The Bald Soprano: An Anti-Play" trans. Donald M. Allen, Masters of Modern Drama, ed. Block and Shedd (1962; New York: Random House, 1963).
3. J.L. Styan, *Modern Drama in Theory and Practice* (Cambridge: Cambridge University Press, 1982), II, p. 125.
4. Robert Brustein, *The Theatre of Revolt* (Boston: Little, Brown, 1964).
5. These examples are respectively from Ionesco's *Rhinoceros,* his *Amédée*, or How to Get Rid of It and Beckett's Endgame.
6. "Absurd Art, Absurd Man, Absurd Heroes" in *The Modern World, III, Reactions*, ed. David Daiches and Anthony Thorlby (London: Aldus Books, 1976), p. 128.
7. Samuel Beckett, *Waiting for Godot*, 2nd ed. (1965; London: Faber and Faber, 1985), pp. 54 and 94.
8. Martin Esslin, *The Pepoled Wound: The Plays of Harold Pinter* (London: Methuen, 1970).
9. Richard Schechner, "Puzzling Pinter," *The Drama Review*, 11 (Winter 1966), p. 184.
10. Alrene Sykes, *Harold Pinter*, p. 25.
11. Harold Pinter, 2nd ed. (London, 1969), pp. 1-2 as quoted by Andrew Kennedy in *Six Dramatists in Search of a Language: Studies in Dramatic Language* (1975; Cambridge: Cambridge University Press, 1976), p. 168.
12. Harold Pinter, *The Birthday Party* (1960; London: Eyre Methuen, 1976), pp. 51-52.
13. Richard Schechner, "Puzzling Pinter," *The Drama Review*, 11 (Winter 1966), p. 178.
14. Jean Vannier, "Theatre of Language," *Tulane Drama Review*, 6 (Spring 1963), p. 182.
15. Qtd. J.L. Styan, *Modern Drama in Theory and Practice*, II, p. 134.
16. John Russell Brown, *A Short Guide to Modern British Drama* (London: Heinemann Educational Books, 1982), p. 15.
17. Harold Pinter, *Old Times* (1971; London: Eyre Methuen, 1972), p. 29.
18. Benedict Nightingale, *An Introduction to 50 Modern British Plays* (London: Pan Books, 1982), pp. 416-17.
19. Tom Stoppard, *Rosencrantz and Guildenstern Are Dead* (1967; London: Faber and Faber, 1984, p. 35.

The Body's Disciplining in Samuel Beckett's *Waiting for Godot*

NISHI CHAWLA

Who perceives, who enunciates the difficulty?
Jacques Derrida, "Cogito and the History of Madness,"
Writing and Difference

Until the subject of a tyrant's will
Became, worse fate, the abject of his own
Percy Bysshe Shelley, *Prometheus Unbound*

In addition to the concern for what constitutes identity, Beckett's writings are also concerned with how the self is disciplined, denigrated, and denied. Beckett's preoccupation with body signifiers reflects his awareness of the regulating and thwarting forces on the body reduced, repressed, and objectified. The repressive nature of impositions on the body, moreover, has political implications for the nature of selfhood. One thing that is noteworthy about Beckett's fictional as well as his dramatic characters is that, very often, they lose all autonomy or ontological status by virtue of this disciplining.

Bodily inscription and the discourse associated with the process of inscribing assume political overtones that, as Sheila Rabillard puts it,

> has essentially to do not with the human being in isolation (if such can in fact be conceived), but with being collective and interpenetrative, each shaped by material and social conditions which each in turn helps to create.[1]

The attacks on the body in Beckett's writings—the wounding, lacerating, incarcerating, maiming—represent a kind of politicization of the body. This political investment of the body is bound up in an intricate reciprocal nexus with the social and other forces operating on the body.

In this article, I will draw on Michel Foucault's *Discipline and Punish*, and to a lesser extent, Elaine Scarry's pioneering work on *The Body in Pain*, to examine in Beckett's *Waiting for Godot*, how political power operates interactively through the use of torture and pain to scrutinize and judge, to bend and break the body. For Foucault, as for Bakhtin, the body itself is the site of ideological inscription. If Bakhtin's work is read as a treatise on bodily semiotics, then the carnivalesque subversion it celebrates forms an interesting dialectical relationship with the bodily disciplining found in the conceptualizations of Foucault. Beckett's obsession with bodily experience stems not only from a concern with Bakhtinian freedom and subversion but also from the Foucauldian idea of power as micro-politics and bodily disciplines. Foucault argues that social and institutional powers, channeled through ideological state violence, transform the individual into an abstraction. The disciplinary mechanisms that repress and thereby define individuality substitute the "calculable" for the "memorable" man, thus producing the self as the object of scientific analysis and control.

In questioning the ontology of the human subject, Beckett subscribes to the Foucauldian view that the subject is an effect of power constituted in discourses that link power to knowledge. The decentering, even the rejection, of human subjectivity as an interior or as essence, and the substitution for it of one fabricated by power and knowledge, has powerful implications in Beckett. In Foucauldian terms,

> the body is also directly involved in a political field; power relations have an immediate hold upon it; they invest it, mark it, train it, torture it, force it to carry out tasks, to perform ceremonies, to emit signs.[2]

Foucault offers a historical argument about the onset of the institutional repression and disciplining of the body. In *Discipline and Punish*, he examines the socio-historical methods by which the Enlightenment spirit of inquiry and truth was used for the surveillance and disciplining of individual bodies. His focus is on conceptions of power-knowledge relations and of the body as the object of the exercise of technologies of power. Within sociological analysis, the body has always assumed the form of a natural body, a body that is without either history or culture. In Foucault's work, on the other hand, the body is a central component in the operation of power relations. His genealogical analysis reveals the body as an object of knowledge and as a target for the exercise of power. The body is shown to be located in a political field, invested with power relations which render it docile and productive, and thus politically and economically useful. Although Foucault's discussion addresses the transformation in forms of punishment and the emergence of the modern penal institutions, the principal focus of analysis falls upon the "power and knowledge relations that invest human bodies and subjugate them by turning them into objects of knowledge" (53). Discipline and training can reconstruct the body to produce new gestures and habits, and ultimately new kinds of people. This political technology of the body has no specific institutional locus. Rather, there is a diffusion of particular technologies of power and their interrelationships with the emergence of those forms of knowledge which have the individual as their subject.

Foucault conceptualizes power neither as an institution nor as a structure but as a "complex strategical situation," as a "multiciplicity of force relations," as simultaneously "intentional" yet "nonsubjective." In short, power is an inherent characteristic of all human relations. And significantly, Foucault has argued that "where there is power, there is resistance" and that power depends for its existence on the presence of a "multiciplicity of points of resistance" (16). By this, Foucault implies that every relationship of power implies a potential "strategy for struggle." He has used the Greek term "agon" for this confrontation. The implication is that the relatively stable mechanisms through which the exercise of power seems to take place may be displaced by the "free play of antagonistic reactions" (37). Within the various discursive levels at which power operates, the exercise of power is also interactive.

One limit to power arises when the subject or individual over which power is exercised is reduced to impotence. The other limit stems from the insubordination, resistance, and consequent freedom of an agent. The relationship between power and the intransigence of freedom is the crucial nexus in the power struggle.

There is a distinct Foucauldian strain in Beckett's work which presents the body as a space on which the tension between self and other, internal and external, is played out. Beckett's writings also represent those beings who endeavour to repress and exercise control over the bodies they can silence. (In this context, W.B. Worthen has discussed at length the corporeal subjection of Beckett's actors, most prominent among whom was Billie Whitelaw performing in *Not I.*) Those who tyrannize deprive the subjected bodies of their elemental rights. Although Foucault is concerned with the historical examination of the biopolitics of power rather than with a Beckettian fictionalized rendering of power, the relevance of Foucault's writings to Beckett's is undeniable. Both can be historically situated in France at the same post-World War II moment. Also, Foucault's writings help us to see the extent to which Beckett's writings are politically engaged, and I shall stress this in the course of my chapter. Foucault's "genealogical" method radically historicizes given patterns and social practices of sexuality and mental ailments as they are controlled by power regimes which have sought to shape, subordinate, suppress, and thereby "naturalize" forms of knowledge. These given patterns of "power/knowledge" emerge in subtle ways in Beckett's writings, which reveal the same hostility as that of Foucault toward the truth-claims of particular regimes as well as the cognitive superiority of their discourses.

The changes in bodily control as part of the "civilizing" process accompanying the development of the capitalist mode of production have been variously commented upon by, among others, Karl Marx, Sigmund Freud, and Norbert Elias. It was Foucault, however, who narrowed the focus from social control to bodily manipulation and control. According to him, the body in pre-industrial times was the vehicle through which the sovereign symbolically projected his power. The body was subject to brute public torture, violence, direct sanctions, executions and mutilations. By the end of the eighteenth century, the body became the focus of various "technologies of power" and increasingly came to be viewed as an instrument for training and manipulation, for extracting energy from it in the most "rational" manner possible. The new control involved, as Foucault says,

> exercising upon [the body] a subtle coercion, of obtaining holds upon it at the level of the mechanism itself—movements, gestures, rapidity and an infinitesimal power over the active body. (*Discipline and Punish*, 137)

The increasing socioeconomic changes, the large-scale "rationalized" systems of production, further brought in a whole new set of "micro-penalties." This led to further refining of body discipline, imposed both from inside and from outside the body.

The key emphasis is on invisible or subtle control: the use of direct coercion has been replaced by indirect coercion in both the private and the public spheres. The effects of these invisible yet pervasive manifestations of power are quite real and it is with these effects—discernible at the level where discourses take hold on bodies and affect the everyday existence of human beings—that Foucault is concerned above all. Foucault describes

> the set of material elements and techniques that serve as weapons, relays, communication routes and supports for the power and knowledge relations that invest human bodies and subjugate them by turning them into objects of knowledge. (28)

Foucault emphasizes not so much power as unitary or imposed from without, or manipulated through a state apparatus endorsing ideological legitimation, as the more subtle impact on the body of institutional discourses. In the conception of the "gaze of power," he provides a basic explanation for the manner in which power is exercised, thus making the connection between power and knowledge. Foucault's discourse on the various "technologies of power" leads to his insistence on material practices operating interactively at the level of everyday social existence. In this way, he has also provided an understanding of relations of power through his analysis of resistance and struggle.

Some of Beckett's plays are absorbing expositions of the visual tyrannizing of the body. In Beckett's drama commencing with *Waiting for Godot*,[3] strategies of surveillance and tyrannizing control are central. The examples of the Chinese torturer in *Eleutheria*, the dumb Lucky and the all-powerful Pozzo in *Godot*, the unnatural "bottling" of the parents in ashbins in *Endgame*, Dan Rooney as the prime child-murder suspect in *All That Fall*, Croak in *Words and Music*, an invisible and sadistic hand in *Act Without Words 1* teasing a mime, the violent attempts at suicide in *Eh Joe*, and the Protagonist's silencing in *Catastrophe* are all paradigmatic cases. The fragmented bodies in his plays, mouth (as in *Not I*) or head suspended in darkness, as well as the stark lighting, costumes and gestures, all focus on Beckett's use of the body as invested with power relations.

A central image of *Waiting for Godot* is that of sado-masochistic bondage. In this play, the bellowing master Pozzo wields his whip over his shackled slave Lucky, who is reduced to a mere pathetic creature, unable to think, to react, or even to know of any existence beyond being bonded to his master. However, being tied to each other by a long rope gives an equivocal dimension to their master-slave relationship: each is linked to the other. Pozzo has many similarities to Moran, who also contemplated tying himself to his son by a rope. Like Moran, Pozzo bullies, smokes (a pipe if not a cigar), dresses well, and eats a good lunch. Eventually Pozzo, like Moran, ends helplessly, "falling to bits."

Pozzo's power is hollow. He is made up of the discourses of power, whose status as *mere* discourses becomes increasingly evident. Initially, Pozzo's theatricality is strident:

> I am Pozzo! (Silence.) Pozzo! . . . Does that name mean nothing to you! (Silence.) I say does that name mean nothing to you? (22)

The flamboyant master exudes force and authority and his encumbered servant displays a cowed submissiveness to him. "I present myself: Pozzo . . . made in God's image!" Styling himself a divinity, Pozzo demands reverential attention. Wielding his whip, Pozzo acts with an overbearing mix of callousness and civility. He brusquely questions the two tramps about Godot and then settles down ostentatiously to relish his dinner. He is full of platitudes about the idea that life is a veil of tears and that one is able to learn something from everyone. He is also full of empty rhetoric, priding himself on his orator's voice, which he cultivates and "inflates" with his atomizer. His speech is replete with imperatives, exclamations, and affected aphorisms alternating between bluster and elocutionary zeal.

That Pozzo is full of insecurities soon becomes evident. With his hyperbolic flourishes, Pozzo appears to be solipsistically content in his make-believe world. He can roar with laughter at the idea of Vladimir and Estragon being his fellows: "Of the same species as Pozzo!" (23), he exclaims. On the other hand, he also appears nervous and vulnerable. He can be lyrical in referring to "torrents of red and white light [which] begin to lose its effulgence, to grow pale" (37), and, alternately, intensely callous to his own slave, even ignoring the alarmed concern of the tramps: "To treat a man . . . like that . . . it's a scandal" (27). Pozzo's disproportionate politeness toward Vladimir and Estragon contrasts with his appropriation of Lucky as worse than an animal. He addresses them as "gentlemen," and the tramps reciprocate his courtesies and apologies. Nonetheless, he displays a more subtle kind of repression in his apparent courtesy. His condescending posture, his supercilious air as well as his inflated gestures complement his sentimental windbaggery, and again form a striking blend of contradictions.

"I am perhaps not particularly human" (19), Pozzo states, "but who cares?" This indifference to one's own human-ness seems to me a desperate attempt at covering a lurking sense of guilt for what he knows to be his hideous actions. Pozzo also has a chronometric obsession as he feverishly calculates the hours of his journey, and often consults his watch, often "cuddling" it to his ear. He is concerned with Estragon's age, and asks the tramps to guess Lucky's age. Intensely time-conscious, when Vladimir states that "Time has stopped," Pozzo protests: "Don't you believe it, sir, don't you believe it. . . . Whatever you like, but not that" (36). Time is of the essence of his contract with himself. Pozzo's melodramatics and literary affectations make him seem to be posturing and speechifying, and his pompous rhetoric assumes shades of grandeur: "I don't like talking in a vacuum" (30). From the start, Pozzo's performance is clearly over-determined, and his authority is revealed to be imposed, factitious not genuine. It is quite evident that Pozzo's oratorical flourishes can make us aware of him as nothing but a collection of discourses.

From within his own comforts, Pozzo hurls monosyllabic orders at Lucky whom he addresses as "Pig" or "Hog," and commands him to hand him his overcoat, hold the whip, and bring the stool or the luncheon basket. While Lucky's plight in responding to the commands, sagging under his weight, or sleeping on his feet at intervals, arouses the tramps' pity, Pozzo remains smugly oblivious to everything but himself. The sheer physical violence involved in Lucky's enslavement is embodied in a kind of circus act. Pozzo is convinced that he does a good act in taking Lucky as his slave instead of "kicking him out on his backside." In spite of Lucky's life-long dedication and service to Pozzo, Pozzo prepares to get rid of him: "such creatures. . . . The best thing would be to kill them" (32). He tells the tramps that he is "bringing him to the fair where I hope to get a good price for him." The master sees to it that no other will exists but his own.

The inevitable reliance of the master upon the slave for his own definition as master is also brought out in the power that Pozzo imposes on Lucky. Pozzo shouts barbaric commands at his slave, on the one hand, and on the other, acknowledges that it is Lucky—"my Lucky"—who had taught him "Beauty, grace, truth of the first water" (33). He knows that he owes it to Lucky, since "[b]ut for him all my thoughts, all my feelings, would have been of common things" (33). Pozzo remarks that it is only by "chance" that he is Lucky's master rather than vice versa, an amusing twist to their sado-masochistic bondage: "Remark that I might just as well have been in his shoes and he in mine."

At the same time, Pozzo's epicureanism is dependent on the continued enslavement of Lucky. Cleverly enough, like a typical despot, he wishes to earn sympathy for himself even as he dismisses Lucky's weeping as undignified. Although Lucky has the wound, "like a goitre" (26) caused by the rope, Pozzo also claims that, in actual fact, it is Lucky who makes him suffer:

> I can't bear it . . . any longer . . . the way he goes on . . . you've no idea . . . it's terrible . . . he must go. . . . I'm going mad. . . . I can't bear it any longer . . . (34)

This is, of course, contradicted by his own confession: "you may be sure there wasn't a word of truth in it" (34). His mannered outburst about the slave "killing him" is more evidence of the emptiness of his own claims to power. One by one, he misplaces his pipe, his atomizer, his precious watch. When Pozzo and Lucky lie tumbled together on the ground, Vladimir calls out the names of both Abel and Cain, and Pozzo responds to both. Significantly, Estragon remarks, "He's all humanity" (83). Drawn into this fabulously calculated self-presentation, the tramps get a glimpse into what the world outside is really like—all spectacle and fixed purpose.

Beckett relentlessly foregrounds the body of the actor as the space on which the tyranny and the operations of power are inscribed. Lucky is burdened with impedimenta he can put down only on Pozzo's command. Lucky enters, his feet shuffling, movements jerky, his panting ceaseless, his body trembling under the weight of basket and Pozzo's baggage. His decrepit body and the running sore on his neck suggest his mental and physical torture. His victimization strangely contrasts with Pozzo's insistence on Lucky's autonomy. If Lucky does not put down his burden, it is because "He wants to impress me, so that I'll keep him" (31). Nonetheless, Pozzo also follows this with: "Well, that's what I think" (31). The inscription of Lucky's marked, silenced body is seen in the fact that his only mode of expression is a body language which speaks hysterically, negating its muted state. Otherwise known as mental atrophy, Lucky's condition is a state of physical palsy, the mind intricately connected to the bodily abjectness. The tramps observe in sheer disgust his "slobber" and his "panting."

There was a time, according to Pozzo, when Lucky could amuse his master by dancing and by thinking; now his dance has deteriorated to a slouch and a totter. If he speaks at all, his speech is uncontrolled and repetitive, the mind losing all bodily control and the body losing all mental control, so much an evidence of instrumental rationalization that the speech barely clutches at a few rudimentary straws of incoherent meaning. Pozzo's instruction, "Think, pig," ensues in a dance as Lucky cannot remember what "think" means, and when he does, he "remember[s]" it as "language." He displays it in a speech which reminds one in a terribly intense manner of the truth of Vladimir's observation that "What is terrible is to have thought." Like Foucault who held that the comprehensive quality of a discourse cannot be identified within a subject, Beckett seems to insist on language as a "decentered totality" where meaning can be drawn only from the relations between signifiers. If knowledge is power, then Lucky's discourse attacks power. Specifically assailing objective knowledge, it also attacks the knowledge on which the two tramps have based their existence, namely of Godot.

The progressive breakdown of all sense or conviction in Lucky's well-known speech is an apt index of the complementarity of mind and body as both are subject to decay and disintegration:

> Given the existence . . . that man in short that man in brief in spite of the strides of alimentation and defecation is seen to waste and pine waste and pine and . . . shrink and dwindle. (42-43)

Rife with contradictions, Lucky's fragmented and unfinished monologue, more a torrent of words, liberates thought from its own tyranny as well as the tyranny of language which communicates the thought. Weaving in and out of the margins of sense, Lucky's "think" mixes sense and nonsense, asyntactical anarchy with flamboyant repetitions in a transgrammatically grotesque discourse. It is not just nonsense pouring out from an automaton. The violence that he seems to be committing on reason offers another (linguistic) version of the violence that he himself has suffered at Pozzo's hands.

In the second act of *Waiting for Godot*, Pozzo is shown as a changed man, blind and given to oracle-like speechifying on time and destiny. He enters the stage with cries asking for help. He appears to be a much gentler and more thoughtful man in both his words and his action. He has shed his histrionic zeal, and collapses on the ground, helpless to raise himself. Gradually and inevitably,

Pozzo's self-definition in his role of a tyrant comes alive to him as really nothing more than a collage of fragmentary voices. Now, significantly, Pozzo is blind and Lucky is dumb. The blind Pozzo is persistently asked when blindness struck him. He replies in extreme agony, "Have you not done tormenting me with your accursed time!" (89). The destroyer destroyed in a mutual sadomasochistic relationship is not really a new phenomenon, and Beckett underlines this fact by foregrounding its ravaging inscription on both the physical and mental dimensions of Pozzo's self. Not only has he lost his memory, he has degenerated in body and mind as well. Begged by the tramps to let the dumb Lucky sing and think once more, Pozzo vents his vexation, and his moments of hysterical groaning culminate in his shouts for help. The truth of his own disintegration dawns on him even as he begins to acknowledge his symbiotic relationship with his victim. The torture that he inflicts on Lucky gradually becomes his own destruction, even as Pozzo is willing to concede that the "good angel" who is "killing" him "used to be so kind . . . so helpful" (34). He is now a "fallen angel" turned "wicked," almost as if the sadomasochistic relationship has turned over on its head.

The flamboyant and bellowing Pozzo and his shackled slave, Lucky, portray a powerful power dynamic. In light of the play's existential theme of lack of freedom, their slave-master relationship does comment on man's constraints. What is man free to do? What is he free to be? More interestingly though, the physical restrictions and scars that Lucky's body suffers as a result of his exploitation by Pozzo comment on the alignment of power and its tyrannizing control of the victim's body. Foucault's analysis of the apparatus of surveillance in the discipline and subjection of bodies relates to the Pozzo-Lucky power equation "in which the techniques that make it possible to see induce effects of power and in which, conversely, the means of coercion make those on whom they are applied, clearly visible" (170). If power insinuates itself into the very discipline constitutive of a rational self, then it is impossible to know rationally one's true humanity independent of power's distorting effects.

In an interesting way, just as Lucky's body has been enslaved to Pozzo, Vladimir and Estragon's minds are enslaved to Godot.

This is endorsed in Act One, when Estragon's repeated question about whether they are "tied to Godot" is interrupted by the appearance of Lucky with a rope around his neck. If Pozzo has been seen by many critics as an incarnation of Godot, it is because both are tyrants and power-wielders. In an early essay, Ronald Gray in fact, insists that Godot has arrived in the image of Pozzo and that the tramps have not recognized him. But Beckett has refused any identification for Godot. Godot has defined the physical and intellectual limits of the two tramps just as much as Pozzo defines Lucky. Vladimir and Estragon cannot leave the spot which has transfixed them. If they "dropped him," they believe "He'd punish us" (59). The limits that define their actions and thoughts are almost violent in effect. The boy-messenger keeps reappearing to comment as cryptically as possible: "No, Sir," "Yes, Sir," "he has a white beard." The tramps, in turn, appear to have no idea what they want of Godot. They make a "request," which becomes an entreaty, "a kind of prayer," "a vague supplication." Quite characteristically Godot makes no reply to the tramps' request since the sovereign can make no terms with his subject. His silence conveys to Vladimir and Estragon the true nature of their situation, namely, that they must only submit.

The risk involved in a futile wait is also emphasized early in the play by the failure to clarify the inexorable conditions set by the hypothetical presence of Mr. Godot. Estragon's "if's"—"And if he doesn't come," "If he came yesterday"—and his "until"—"until he comes"—project the anxieties existing in this act of waiting for Godot. As they "canter" about Godot, Vladimir is forced to acknowledge the very real fact that they no longer have any "rights." The overwhelming nature of their apprehension of Godot is suggested by the fact that even the slightest noise, the wind in the reeds or a shout, brings a nameless fear, as if ushering in the coming of Godot. The cry that precedes the arrival of Pozzo and Lucky creates the illusion of Godot's arrival: "Godet. . . . Godot. . . . Godin" (29). The name of Godot is silenced with profuse apologies for having mistaken Pozzo for "him": "Personally I wouldn't even know him if I saw him." The uncertainty and dread about Godot's appearance are offset by such remarks to Pozzo as: "Tell him . . . tell him you saw us." Waiting makes urgent demands even when those who wait begin to lose that sense of urgency. The ritual act of passing the time loses meaning, and the silences become interminably unendurable. Vladimir's hallucination, "It's Godot! At last!" and Estragon's, "Do you think God sees me?" suggest despair and no-exit.

Vladimir and Estragon's fearful sense of anticipation of Godot who has completely swamped their thoughts forms an analogue of the terror that is embodied in Lucky's servile relationship with his master. The tramps' idle chatter acting as an evasive symptom of the unnamed fear of Godot results in the final panic-stricken cry, "I'm in hell." The pathos of Lucky's role—the kicks and counter-kicks, his physical enslavement, aphasia and breakdown of thoughts—is a result of Pozzo's constant brutality. The two pairs, Vladimir and Estragon and Pozzo and Lucky find a point of fusion in Beckett's thematic rendition of tyranny.

To come back to Foucault who demonstrated in his *Discipline and Punish* the marks of the legal inscription of culpability on the malefactor's body, we see how the Foucauldian polemic pervades the world of Lucky and Pozzo in *Godot.* Whether discoursing on prisons, sex, or madness, the central thrust of Foucault's writings is the body as the most proximate and immediate aspect of one's being, as a necessary feature of social location and personal "enselfment." Bodies are the surface of emergence for penality. Indeed, the whole point of the opening chapter, "The body of the condemned," in *Discipline and Punish* can be said to be the centering of the body within a political economy of punishment:

> The body now serves as an instrument or intermediary: if one intervenes upon it to imprison it, or to make it work, it is in order to deprive the individual of a liberty that is regarded both as a right and a property. The body, according to this penality, is caught up in system of constraints and privations, obligations and prohibitions. Physical pain, the pain of the body itself, is no longer the constituent element of the penality. (10-11)

The body-punishment nexus is registered in the way Beckett's characters constantly experience what Foucault refers to as the "political economy" of the body. Foucault's distinction between the "intelligible" body represented through discourse and the "docile-useful body" disciplined by social control shows the dual relationship between bodies and their representation. For Foucault, the body is a referential field of signifiers which refuses any distinct and independent sense of individuality, at the same time that it becomes inundated with ulterior meaning. And in Beckett's writings too, the body does not expose the power that a dominant group or culture exerts, as much as the effect wrought through its machinations on the body. Lucky's body is a transparency through which the impressions of his repressed and thwarted consciousness become visible.

The misfits and eccentrics in Beckett's work are distortions of the human body, outrageously bizarre descriptions of the human physiognomy. Schizophrenics, aphasiacs, neurasthenics, dysfunctional beings with phantom limbs—the disfigured and disturbed beings are often indicative of the warping effects on the bodily. What is remarkable about Beckett's fictional as well as his dramatic characters is that very often, they are unable to possess any autonomy or an ontological status. The various forms of tyrannizing of the body, social, familial, ideological, and political, undermines the notion of a stable, teleological notion of the self.

After *Godot*, there are many android creatures in Beckett's writings who reflect Beckett's attitude to the status of selfhood when the sentient body is repressed. In this context, the extremely useful work done by Anna McMullan studies Beckett's later drama in order to show how

> the body is foregrounded as a locus of the struggle for control and mastery, either within the subject who has internalized the laws of identity and authority, or between the subject and the external modes of law and discipline. (17)

Beckett's ontologically mongrelized creatures endeavour to break with and transcend the Cartesian dualisms of body and mind, subject and object. As part of their material reality, however, they experience the material conditions of social existence which are inscribed on their bodies. Once their sensory capacities are thwarted and contract, the embodied subject is displaced by the body as object. As the body is subjected to external repressions, this is the necessary concomitant of the loss of a comprehensible structure which relates one to the world. The indeterminacy of bodily being results from the erasure of identity as it is prescribed and proscribed, disguised and disciplined by political configurations of an increasingly techno-powered world. In this sense, subjectivity cannot be understood as a phenomenon of the essential, interior self, but as an effect of power which has been inscribed upon the body's surface.

The farcical comicality of distorted and automated bodily attitudes is an inherent feature of Beckett's drama, reflecting the relationship between the framework of disciplining and its impact on the body. In *Endgame*, Hamm's body functions are reduced in the extreme: immobilized in his chair, he seems paralyzed, and is also blind. Nagg and Nell grotesquely parody physical impotence and emotional repression. The room itself takes the shape of a "cranial box" where the mind has been blocked and caged. In the play, the dustbins in which Hamm's parents, Nagg and Nell reside are synecdochically associated with the corporeal body of man since man enters life and departs from it in the form of what Murphy calls a "waste product" of the organic processes.

In *Krapp's Last Tape*, the technical apparatus of the tape recorder as a machine becomes one with Krapp's various selves, the younger versions of Krapp, so alike and yet so different from the older Krapp. Beckett instructed the actor Pierre Chabert, in his 1975 Paris production of the play, "to become as much as possible one body with the machine." The relationship between Krapp and the tape is a physical, even a visceral one as Krapp responds to it as a sensual object, body to body. Through the mechanical device of the tape-recorder, Krapp replaces his physical desires with the reason and mind of the gadget. *Krapp's Last Tape*, like the later *Words and Music*, takes off from Proust's vision of the changing self as Krapp talks to another version of himself, his recorded voice from thirty years earlier. In *Play*, Beckett manipulates the spotlight as an arbitrary mechanism of control over the three rigidified heads who are immersed in their own individual revelations of the truth of their lives. Underlying this strategic "play," is of course, the disruption and cleaving of the mind from the body. Beckett's foregrounding of the body situated between human and animal, organism and machine, results in a techno-organic, humanoid hybrid man. Beckett ridicules and flouts Descartes's positioning of the human self above its own body by its ability to think as well as articulate thoughts. It is in this sense that the body and the machine interact in the hybridized world of Beckett, and the body is "rewritten" by the disciplining of the technologies of the self. The body thus becomes a political surface which is distinct from the anatomical body.

NOTES

1. Sheila Rabillard, "The Body in Beckett: Dene-gation and the Critique of a Depoliticized Theatre," *Criticism*, Vol. 34, No. 1 (Winter 1992), p. 99.
2. Michel Foucault, *Discipline and Punish* (London: Penguin, 1977), p. 25.
3. Samuel Beckett, *Waiting for Godot* (New York: Grove Press, 1954).

Samuel Beckett's *Endgame*: A Game That Never Ends

MANOJ G. BHISE

The first performance of *Endgame* in Great Britain was given in French under its original title *Fin de Partie* at the Royal Court Theatre, London, on 3rd April 1957. It was directed by Roger Blinn, who also played the role of Hamm, the protagonist. Incidentally, Beckett dedicated this play to him. The play was not only well received by the audience, but also generated greater comments than Beckett's earlier play *Waiting for Godot*. It was so due to the most shattering experience that Beckett had shared with his audience of the time. In this play, Beckett has depicted his strange, queer inexplicable vision of the end of the world. The researcher had an opportunity to play the role of Hamm in the play-reading performance organised by the Department of English, University of Poona in 1989.

Endgame depicts a ritual of agony. There is a vision of the approaching end of civilisation. All the four characters are handicapped in some way or the other. Hamm is blind and cannot stand up. Clov is stiff and cannot sit down. He is an attendant to Hamm, who is seen in the wheelchair throughout the play. Hamm's legless parents—Nagg, the father, and Nell, the mother—are kept in the ashbins. All the four characters are the survivors of the human race living in Hamm's house, outside which is death. According to Ruby Cohn, they are the 'monsters of awareness.'[1]

The play takes place in a bare interior, with two small windows high up. The light inside is grey indicating that the life inside is going to be extinguished very soon. In the centre of the room sits the protagonist Hamm, who is blind and immobile. He wears a skull-cap. His face is covered with a blood-stained handkerchief. When the curtain goes up, everything is motionless. Clov, Hamm's attendant uncovers the two windows, uncovers the ashbins and uncovers Hamm. The audience takes time to see Nagg and Nell in the ashbins. Clov's opening remarks set the mood of the play.

> Finished, it's finished, nearly finished, it must be nearly finished.[2]

Thus the basic dramatic situation is very simple. Hamm is slowly dying. In order to pass time till death eventually overpowers him, he tries to complete a long story. It is a story Hamm has been working on for quite some time. Beckett has not made it clear whether this story is fictitious or based on real events. Hamm calls it his 'chronicle.' (121) It is the story of a man crawling towards him on his belly and with the intention of getting some help for himself and his little boy. When the man asks for bread or corn in order to revive his boy, Hamm tantalises him, describing "a nice pot of porridge—a nice pot and a half of porridge, full of nourishment." (118) But instead of fulfilling his expectation, Hamm dashed them violently: "use your head, can't you, use your head, you're on earth, there is no cure for that." (97) The boy in this story could be related to the boy who appears at the end of the play—a symbol of fertility and energy.

Both inside and outside the house, decay has already started. Nell, Hamm's mother probably dies during the play, but it is not made clear. There is "no more nature." (97) There are no more sugar plums, no more sawdust, no more rugs and no more painkillers. Time has slowed down to a stop for all those who are inside. Clov says,

> All life long the same questions, the same answers. (93)

As a result of the slowing down of time, they have no 'future' to think of. They have memories of the 'past' which they can recall and be happy or sad. 'Present' is meant only for suffering. They have no choice except to wait for the doomsday. In their situation there is no Godot to their rescue. Death is the only certainty that can put an end to their anguish. In the game of chess what Hamm can do is to try at the most, to postpone the end. His apprehensions can be seen in the following dialogue.

> And yet I hesitate, I hesitate to . . . to end. Yes, there it is, it's time it ended and yet I hesitate to . . . to end. (93)

Thus all the survivors of this chess board—Hamm as King, Clov as Knight, Nagg and Nell as rooks—are going to be exterminated. Hamm firmly believes that living means suffering, that is why when a flea is found on Clov's person, Hamm asks him to kill it "for the love of God." (108) 'Love for God' means to relieve the creatures of this earth, and thus from their sufferings.

Clov decides many times to leave Hamm, but he cannot do so. It is as if they are wedded to each other. But time comes when he takes a firm decision to leave Hamm's skull-like room. There are several references during the play to the idea that some kind of change is taking place. For instance, Hamm asks Clov, "What's happening?" Clov replies: "Something is taking its course." (133)

The appearance of a little boy is a miracle. As such birth from nothing cannot be exterminated, Hamm submits himself to the situation. He cannot control the game between him and time. The very sight of the boy is a checkmate to Hamm. There is a possibility, not for Hamm but for Clov that life may be renewed. Whether he leaves Hamm or not is an unending question because in the stage direction Beckett says:

> He halts by the door and stands there impassive and motionless, his eyes fixed on Hamm till the end. (93)

The most striking thing about the structure of *Endgame* is that Beckett has taken all the care that the audience should not get involved in the sentimental world of the play. His protagonist Hamm makes it clear at the outset that what follows is taking place in a play. "Me—to play Old Stancher! (107) Again the same declaration comes as if to remind the audience that what happened was a play.

Clov: Why this farce day by day?
Hamm: Routine—one never knows . . . (93)

The play initially was in two Acts. The Second Act was distinctly shorter than the first. Later on, Beckett reduced the play to one full-length Act. In the bare interior under grey light, Hamm, his father Nagg, mother Nell and his attendant son Clov stay together. Though all of them are waiting for the end, only one death is reported indirectly in the play, that of Nell. It is a day like any other day at the beginning, but as the play heads towards the end, it becomes clear that it is not a usual, normal day. Everything and everybody starts 'running down.' After Nell's death, Nagg becomes silent. Hamm's sedatives are exhausted. Outside the room is 'corpsed' world and the inside of the room is going to be 'corpsed' very soon.

Thus, Beckett has designed a different kind of structure in *Endgame*. A certain symmetry can be observed in the prolonged single Act of *Endgame*, prolonged stories of Hamm and prolonged end of a game. The play begins and ends with Hamm's face covered with the same blood-stained handkerchief and his utterance 'old stancher!' (132)

In the atmosphere outside and in the desolate condition inside the room, there is a gradual exhaustion of everything—from sugar plums to coffins. It is a downward progress in the sense that Beckett has used 'game' as a metaphor which is associated with the word 'end,' and so it is a downward progress. There are two breaking points where physically the only active supporter of Hamm, Clov, decides to leave him at the end and secondly where psychologically speaking, Clov realises that he has been deliberately made to suffer so much that he loses faith in friendship, beauty and life itself. Because of this awareness, he can see the possibility of a different life outside, and even if there is death outside, he is prepared to die.

> I open the door of the cell and go. I am so bowed I only see my feet, if I open my eyes, and between my legs a little trail of black dust. . . . It's easy going . . . when I fall I'll weep for happiness. (129)

The appearance of a boy is an unexpected happening. Neither the audience nor even Hamm nor Clov is mentally prepared to accept it. Clov and the audience take it as a pleasant surprise, whereas Hamm takes it as a shock. Perhaps *Endgame* is the only play in which Beckett has pointed out a new path of hope, vision, and life. One like Clov may muster up courage to explore this possibility. Perhaps with this note, at the end of the play, Beckett goes very close to the existentialist view of life.

The entire action of the play has been reduced to words. The play is conceived thoroughly in theatrical terms. The play is less dramatic and more performance oriented. In every scene, the visual and sound effects are woven into the verbal text. In the same manner, the action of the play also runs through at a very slow pace through words. The audience has been given a slight indication as to what they are going to watch. In the process, everybody, including Hamm, is prepared for death. Nell has already been out of question. Nagg has fallen silent, Clov is leaving the place, preferably to die outside. Even Hamm covers his face with the bloodstained handkerchief and sits motionless.

Thus, there is no action like the action of any well-made play. Physical action is impossible because all the characters are immobile. Clov can move with his queer walk, but he is stiff. He can move wall to wall and push the wheel chair of Hamm to take a round. He is the only character who at least can move from one place to another, though with great difficulty. By the command of his master, he has extinguished everything 'living' outside. So, looking through the telescope very often, reporting it to the master and as and when ordered, taking his master for a round of the room—that is all that he does at the master's call by whistle. So, physically, there is no action to speak of. Nagg and Nell, the legless parents of Hamm, have been passive throughout.

This kind of action on the psychological level is not new to Beckett's readers and viewers. Playing games, inventing stories and passing time are the recurring features of his plays.

With a recurrent interest in psychological behaviour, modern drama tends to put a greater emphasis on character. But 'absurd' plays like Ionesco's *The Leader* or Pinter's *The Caretaker* or *The Homecoming* and all plays of Beckett, which are specifically concerned with the inner working of the human mind, do not embody characters who can be identified with the people in the real world. In *Endgame* Hamm and Clov represent opposite psychological tendencies, but it would be misleading to think of them as fully developed personalities. In fact, Beckett's characters are always seen lacking in physique. They are unable either to be seen or move or hear or to see. Hamm is blind. Krapp in *Krapp's Last Tape* is deaf. *Endgame* is like a gallery of cripples. Clov cannot sit, Nagg and Nell are legless and are kept in the ashbins.

The theme of domination and subservience is central to Beckett's plays, especially in plays like *Endgame*. Hamm, who can talk fluently, dominates Clov, Nagg and Nell, who are comparatively less articulate. At one point Clov asks him:

> There is one thing I'll never understand. Why I always obey you. Can you explain that to me?

Hamm uses all bad adjectives for his father:

Hamm: Accursed progenitor!
Nagg: One pap!
Hamm: The old folks at home! No decency left!
Nagg: I want me pap?
Hamm: Accursed fornicator

Beckett's use of language probes the limitation of language both as a means of communication and as a means of expression. Perhaps the theatre is the medium through which he tries to find means of expression beyond language.

Silence basically is an essential aspect of any individual attempt to cope with an inner uncertain self and the disorder outside it. Beckett has brought this aspect effectively in the theatre. John Russell Brown, while elaborating on this point in his *Beckett and the Art of the Nonplus,* says: "Silence had been used previously only with elaborate supporting devices or only for the most fleeting effects. But Beckett has used both silence and words with such authority that today almost every dramatist follows his lead confidently."

Throughout the play, the dialogue reflects the pointless to-and-fro of everyday conversation. This effect is achieved by silences and pauses. Interestingly, in *Endgame*, Beckett's dialogues are characterised by asking questions, mostly by Hamm. In the first forty exchanges of the play, Hamm asks Clov as many as twenty-seven questions. Sometimes his questions begin with a pause and Clov's answers also end with a pause.

These silences and pauses help Beckett to show a drift between the characters. It also shows noncommunication amongst them and thirdly considering *Endgame* as a metaphor, Beckett shows their steady moves till the end. Most of the time, Hamm does not listen to Clov. He is plunged into his own thoughts. The play ends with Hamm covering his face with a blood-stained handkerchief. When asked whether Hamm covers his face in order to die, Beckett replies:

> No, only the better to be able to be silent

The concept of time for Beckett, like days, weeks, months and years have lost their essential meaning and so 'yesterday' for Clov is

> That bloody awful day before today.

In order to understand the realism in *Endgame*, one has to study how Beckett has reproduced the inner working of the mind of Hamm and Clov. Beckett has presented these two characters with their thoughts and impressions as and when they occur, without any rearrangement. That precisely is the working of the Absurdists, as far as realism is concerned. Hamm's role-playing is a part of this realism. He is aware of himself as an actor, not in a metaphorical sense but in reality. He is actually on the stage—the stage which is his reality and Beckett's text is his destiny. Hence he answers Clov's question in a theatrical language:

Clov: What is there to keep me here?
Hamm: The dialogue.

Ruby Cohn points out, examining this aspect in a number of Beckett's plays as, "unique in its relentless focus upon the play as play."[3] From both, literal and literary meaning, Beckett has shown the ultimate realities of the two worlds. In a way they are different, but both of them lead to an empty world.

There is a symmetry in the setting which is again a unique feature of Beckett. Two windows, two ashbins, two couples—Nagg and Nell, as husband and wife, and Hamm and Clov, as master and servant or father and son. Beckett has beautifully balanced (to show the imbalance) the interior of the house. Two windows are 'high up' that look at the world outside and two low ashbins which have caged an old generation. In the centre of the stage is Hamm, the master, the owner, the knight, the landlord of the shelter. He is the lord or the king without amenities! Revolving around him is crippled Clov. The empty space of the stage is filled up by pain, agony, suffering! Death is preferable to this suffering, but Hamm hesitates to end and *Endgame* ends without end.

NOTES

1. Ruby Cohn, *Back to Beckett* (New Jersey: Princeton University Press, 1973), p. 140.
2. *Endgame* in *Complete Dramatic Works* (London: Faber and Faber, 1986), p. 93.
3. Ruby Cohn, "Play and Player in the Plays of Samuel Beckett," *Yale French Studies*, 29, 1962, p. 44. Qtd. *Journal of Beckett Studies*, Vol. IV, Spring 1979, p. 52.

The Speech Act Theory and the Analysis of Drama

SHRIDHAR B. GOKHALE

Drama as a literary genre is distinguished from poetry and fiction in that it exclusively employs the dialogic mode. There may be dialogue in fiction but the genre typically employs the narrative mode. In most novels and short stories, narration is interspersed with dialogue. Poetry rarely uses dialogue. Dramatic dialogue usually does not report about actions on or off the stage; it constitutes dramatic action itself. The action in the play is perceived and appreciated through the medium of language. Devices like setting and music undoubtedly play a significant role in drama, but still they are subservient to the words. That accounts for the fact that in most plays words are more dramatic than action.

The concept 'language as action' is the most significant contribution of the Speech Act Theory proposed originally by Austin[1] and developed by him in collaboration with Searle. The conventional philosophical view of language is that the use of language consists of a set of propositions about the world including different actions in it. Austin originally proposed that at least some language does not consist of propositions. That is, it does not perform the informative function. For example, when the Registrar of marriages says to a couple, 'I hereby declare you to be husband and wife,' he does not make a statement about the reality of the world, but he performs the action of effecting the marriage and giving it legal status. The act of utterance is simultaneous with and indistinguishable from the act of the couple's marriage. This is clear from the fact that a minute before the utterance, the couple are unmarried, but after the utterance, they are already married.

According to Austin's earlier position, utterances may be divided into constatives and performatives, Constatives are statements about the world like 'It rained heavily yesterday' and—performatives are utterances performing different actions like 'I allow you to leave early.' According to Austin's later position, all the utterances are necessarily performatives in that even the most neutral and descriptive statements perform some action in the context given.

According to the standard version of the Speech Act theory, an utterance in a context can be analyzed at three different levels, because three different speech acts are simultaneously performed. The locutionary act consists in saying something which is meaningful and something which can be understood by the listener. The locutionary act is concerned with the literal or superficial meaning of an utterance. The illocutionary act consists in doing something through the act of utterance itself. It is concerned with the question of the speaker's intention in saying something. It also deals with the implied meaning(s) of an utterance. Incidentally, what is unsaid is often more significant than what is said directly. The perlocutionary act consists in the effect that an utterance has on the listener and the appropriate response on the listener's part. Elam distinguishes between the illocutionary act and the perlocutionary act by suggesting that the former refers to "the act performed *in* saying something, such as asking a question, ordering someone to do something, promising, asserting the truth of a proposition, etc." (158) and the latter refers to the act "performed *by means of* saying something, such as persuading someone to do something, convincing one's interlocutor, moving him to anger, and so on."[2] For example, if someone says to another person in a specific context, 'I am thirsty,' the utterance can be understood or analyzed at three levels. As a locutionary act, it communicates that the speaker experiences a particular physical state and that he needs water or some other drink. At the level of the illocutionary act, the speaker might be requesting that they should move to another place where water is easily available. The perlocutionary act consists in the listener's action like bringing a glass of water or making enquiries regarding the sources of water, etc.

Elam emphasizes the role of speech acts in the dynamics of drama. According to him, "It is this social, interpersonal, executive power of language, the pragmatic 'doing things with words,' which is dominant in the drama. Dramatic discourse is a network of complementary and conflicting illocutions and perlocutions." (159)

Let us illustrate the usefulness and also a limitation of the study of speech acts in the analysis of drama with reference to a dramatic dialogue from Samuel Beckett's celebrated play *Waiting for Godot.*

Estragon: Let's go.
Vladimir: We can't.
Estragon: Why not?
Vladimir: We're waiting for Godot.

The most important observation about this dramatic dialogue that any stylistic analysis would make is that it is repeated a number of times throughout the text. The dialogue is foregrounded and is significant to a stylistician. The recurrence of these sentences seems to add to their 'significance-weight.'

Estragon's initial utterance 'let's go,' as a locutionary act, brings out its basic literal meaning and is to be understood in the context of the fact that Estragon and Vladimir have been waiting at the same place for a long time and nothing significant has happened. The illocutionary act that Estragon performs through this utterance is that of making a suggestion regarding a possible course of action. The perlocutionary act expected by Estragon is perhaps that Vladimir should agree to move away from the place. However, Vladimir's response indicates rejection of Estragon's suggestion. That is the illocutionary act performed through Vladimir's pithy locution 'We can't'. Estragon responds to this by asking the question 'Why not?' This has the force of a rhetorical question and an assertive statement 'We can certainly go.' The perlocutionary act expected by Estragon at this point is that Vladimir should agree to go. Instead, Vladimir reminds Estragon of something that both of them know very well. That is the illocutionary act performed through Vladimir's utterance.

What is presented in the preceding paragraph is a tentative analysis of the first occurrence of the dialogue in the play using the Speech Act Theory. However, a more interesting question is whether the same speech acts are performed by the two speakers concerned, when exactly the same dialogue is repeated verbatim a number of times in the play. Obviously, a repeated dialogue cannot be analyzed in the same terms as the first occurrence of a dialogue. The repetition introduces the element of a 'ritualistic' conversational exchange, which ceases to be a conversational exchange in the true sense of the term. A question is normally asked when there is a gap in the speaker's information and when he wants the gap to be filled in. But the repeated question 'Why not' ceases to be a question and the repeated reminder 'We're waiting for Godot' ceases to be a reminder. In other words, there is a 'rupture' of communication in the sense the dialogue ceases to convey any 'new' information either to the participants of the dialogue or the audience. The dialogue is 'frozen' because the various speech acts cease to be performed through the use of language. This 'stylization' of language contributes to the effect of absurdity in the play.

It may be concluded that though the Speech Act Theory certainly offers us a valuable framework in which dramatic dialogues can be fruitfully analyzed, there may be cases in creative literature like the recurrence of identical dialogue discussed above which may not be analyzable in terms of the theory to account for their effect and effectiveness.

NOTES

1. J.L. Austin, *How to Do Things with Words* (London: Oxford University Press, 1962).
2. K. Elam, *The Semiotics of Theatre and Drama* (London: Methuen, 1980), p. 158.

Recurrent Motifs in Harold Pinter's *The Room*, *The Dumb Waiter* and *The Birthday Party*

PRABHANJAN B. MANE

In 1953 at the Theatre de Babylone in Paris, Samuel Beckett play called *En Attendant Godot* (*Waiting for Godot*) appeared. And the literary world was surprised and shocked by this drama which was so different from the traditional 'well-made' drama that it created the term "Theatre of the Absurd." This movement known as the Theatre of the Absurd or Absurdist Movement was not a consciously conceived movement, and it has never had any clear-cut philosophical doctrines and no meetings. Each of the main playwrights of the movement seems to have developed independently of each other. The playwrights most often associated with this movement are Samuel Beckett, Eugene Ionesco, Jean Genet, Arthur Adamov, Harold Pinter and Edward Albee.

The Absurd drama reflects the attitude that the universe is without purpose and that human life is futile and meaningless. Under such circumstances, man's existence becomes absurd. In both form and content, the theatre of the absurd portrays human beings as isolated from others.

The title "Theatre of the Absurd" comes not from a dictionary-definition of the word 'absurd,' but from Martin Esslin's book *The Theatre of the Absurd.* In this book, he says: "The Theatre of the Absurd represents trends that have been apparent in the more esoteric kinds of literature since the 1920s or in painting since the first decade of this century."[1] This trend, sometimes, described as a search for novelty, combines a number of very ancient and highly respectable modes of literature and theatre of the contemporary situation of Western man. The Absurd plays, which are so often superciliously dismissed as nonsense or mystification, 'have' something to say and 'can' be understood. These plays are part of a new and still developing stage conventions that have not yet been generally understood and have hardly ever been defined. Inevitably, plays written in this new convention will be regarded as impertinent and outrageous impostures. If a good play must have a cleverly constructed story, these have no story or plot to speak of; if a good play is judged by subtlety of characterization and motivation, these are often without recognizable characters and present the audience with almost mechanical puppets; if a good play has to have a fully explained theme, which is neatly exposed and finally solved, these often have neither a beginning nor an end; if a good play is said to hold the mirror upto nature and portray the manners and mannerisms of the age in finely observed sketches, these seem often to be reflections of dreams and nightmares; if a good play relies on witty repartee and pointed dialogue; these often consist of incoherent babblings. These plays are quite different from those of the conventional play and therefore use quite different methods. They can be judged only by the stantards of the Theatre of the Absurd.

The term 'absurd,' observes Esslin, "originally means 'out of harmony' in a musical context." Its dictionary definition is 'out of harmony with reason or propriety, incongruous, illogical, unreasonable.' In common speech the word 'absurd' may simply mean 'ridiculous.' But Ionesco defines the term as: "which is devoid of purpose . . . cut off from his religious, metaphysical and transcendental roots, man is lost; all his affections become senseless, absurd, useless." Theatre of the Absurd strives to express its sense of the senselessness of the human condition and the inadequacy of the rational approach by the open abandonment of rational devices and discursive thought.

Jean-Paul Sartre in his book *Existentialism and Humanism* says that for the Absurdists the modern world is a godless world. This is the modern system of belief made famous by Sartre in the 1940 in which the world is meaningless and each person is alone and completely responsible for his own actions by which he makes his own character.

Harold Pinter's absurd play *The Birthday Party*[2] is a curious mixture of his first two one-act plays *The Room* and *The Dumb Waiter*. These one-act plays contain some of the basic themes and a great deal of the very personal style and idiom of Pinter's later and more successful work i.e. *The Birthday Party.*

In *The Room*, a woman called Rose talks while she prepares food for her husband, Bert, a silent van driver. Rose and Bert are interrupted by the landlord, Kidd, with whom she talks at cross purposes. After he leaves, Bert goes for a run in his van. Soon she is interrupted by Mr. and Mrs. Sands who claim to be apartment-hunters. Seeking the landlord, they meet, in the dark basement, a man who tells them of a vacancy: the flat where Rose and Bert live. After the Sands depart, Kidd returns, pleading with Rose to receive the man in the basement who wants to see her alone. Kidd's earlier visit was to discover whether Bert had gone. The visitor is a blind Negro named Riley who tells Rose that her father wants her to come home, and who calls her Sal. Bert returns to find them together. He knocks Riley to the floor, strikes him, and kicks his head against the stove until he lies still—possibly dead. Rose then cries out that she is blind. The suspense created by the elementary ingredients of pure, pre-literary theatre: a stage, two people, a door; a poetic image of an undefined fear and expectation. When asked by a critic what the two people in the room are afraid of, Pinter replied, "Obviously they are scared of what is outside the room. Outside the world there is a world bearing upon them which is frightening. I am sure it is frightening to you and me as well." Thus, the room, which is the centre and chief poetic image of the play, is one of the recurring motifs of Pinter's work.

The Dumb Waiter, also in one act, uses the same basic situation as *The Room*. Again, we are in a room enclosed by a dark, mysterious world outside. Again, the people in the room are watching, in dreadful suspense, a door which is certain to open. Moreover, in this case we are, from quite an early point in the play, made aware of the fact that whoever enters by the door will have to die, for the two people in the room are professional assassins. *The Dumb Waiter* revolves around two people in a room. Whereas *The Birth-*

day Party chiefly focuses on the victim, *The Dumb Waiter* centres upon victimizers—two hired killers, Ben and Gus—who wait for instructions as to when their victim will enter. While they wait, they read a newspaper, they bicker over details, and one of them—to the other's annoyance—frequently asks questions. Strange events occur, such as an envelope sliding under a door. More mysteriously, the dumb waiter clatters down with orders for food. When Gus goes out to get a glass of water, the speaking tube near the dumb waiter comes to life again. Ben gets his final instructions (or orders) from above. They are to kill the next man who enters. It is Gus, his colleague, who is the next victim. He is stripped of jacket, waistcoat, tie, holster and revolver. On this tableau the curtain closes. In any case: the variation on the opening situation of *The Room* is brilliantly ingenious and intelligent. Rose in 'her' room, looking at 'her' door, was clearly a victim-to-be. Ben and Gus are looking at the door waiting for the victim to walk in the trap.

Pinter's first full-length play, *The Birthday Party* combines some of the characters and situations of *The Room* and *The Dumb Waiter*. As in *The Room*, *The Birthday Party* has a character (this time male) who fears intrusion from without. Stanley Webber, a man in his late thirties, indolent and apathetic, has somehow found refuge in the house of Meg and Petey Boles, in a seaside town. He seems not to have left it since he arrived the year before Goldberg and McCann arrive, brutally interrogate him, break his eyeglasses, crush his spirit, drive him to a break-down following which he cannot speak coherently and take him away with them. Goldberg has an affair with Lulu, a neighbour, but McCann turns her away when her presence interrupts their activities with Stanley. Pinter does not reveal why Stanley is living in the lodging house or why the intruders do what they do.

True to its title, *The Birthday Party* contains a birthday party for Stanley, who insists it is not his birthday. Birthday not only means the anniversary of one's birth, it also means the day of one's birth, and in *The Birthday Party* the celebration of the former helps to create the latter. The intruders turn Stanley into what McCann calls a new man. At their hands he is reborn, made into a different kind of person on a birthday that becomes a birth-anniversary!

When *The Birthday Party* opened in the United States, a lady attended the theatre. But she could make no sense of the play. So, she wrote a letter to Pinter: "Dear Sir, I would be obliged if you would kindly explain to me the meaning of your play *The Birthday Party*. These are the points which I do not understand.—1. Who are the two men? 2. Where did Stanley come from? 3. Were they all supposed to be normal? You will appreciate that without the answers to my questions I cannot fully understand your play." Pinter replied in kind: "Dear Madam, I would be obliged if you kindly explain to me the meaning of your letter. These are the points which I do not understand: 1. Who are you? 2. Where do you come from? 3. Are you supposed to be normal? You will appreciate that without the answers to my questions I cannot fully understand your letter." Implicitly Pinter answered the woman's questions. By responding to her in precisely the same terms in which she responded to his characters, he invited her to respond to his characters in the same terms in which he responded to a real human being.

The safe and warm haven of *The Room*, menaced by an intrusion from the cold outside world, has here become a dingy seaside boarding house. This resort is kept by a simple, slovenly but motherly (or elderly) old woman, Meg, who has many of the features of Rose in *The Room*. Rose is not a mother, but she is the prototype of all Pinter's chattering, fussing, nagging mother figures, the women who never stop to listen but never stop asking implicitly for the goodwill of the husband or son or lodger. The beginning of the play is very much like that of *The Room* with Petey, like Bert, sitting at the breakfast table with a paper, without uttering a word, while Meg, like Rose, prattles on with her suffocating mixture of motherly attentiveness and self-praise. Both Meg and Rose talk about the food they are giving their husbands.

Meg I've got your cornflakes ready. (She disappears and reappears.)
Here's your cornflakes.
Petey Very Nice.
Meg I thought that they'd be nice. (She sits at the table.)

Like Rose's chatter to Bert, Meg's fussy attentiveness shows the wish to give and receive attention combined with an insulting reduction of the grown man to the status of a little boy.

Meg's husband, Petey, is almost as silent as Rose's husband Bert in *The Room*. But he lacks Bert's brutality. He is a kind old man, employed as a deck-chair attendant on the promenade. Petey, like Bert, hardly talks, lets himself be pampered by his wife, and goes out of the house for long periods. But while Bert is savage and brutal, Petey is mild. Bert's brutality reappears in that of Goldberg and McCann. In other words, one figure has been split into three components.

The two emissaries of a mysterious and brutal organization who arrive to watch Stanley away from Meg—a Jew Goldberg, and an Irishman, McCann—have a good deal in common, both in their function and in their manner of operation, with the two hired killers in *The Dumb Waiter*. But these characters have become far more complex in the three-act play. Ben and Gus, the two gunmen of *The Dumb Waiter*, reappear as a sinister pair of strangers—an Irishman, brutal and silent, and a Jew, full of false 'bonhomie' and spurious worldly wisdom. Like Ben and Gus, they are two agents working for some organization we know nothing about, but although their mission and its motives remain mysterious, their language and their behaviour merge perfectly well into the rest of the play. As in the two earlier plays, the door opens. Two sinister visitors, Goldberg and McCann, want a room in Meg's boarding house. It soon becomes clear that they are after Stanley. Are they emissaries of some secret organization he has betrayed? or male nurses sent out to fetch him back to an asylum he has escaped from? or emissaries from another world like the blind Negro in *The Room*? This question is never answered. We don't know whether Stanley is going to be killed or not, but the way Goldberg speaks about 'doing the job' constantly reminds us of the two gunmen in *The Dumb Waiter*; while the way he speaks about how he was given the job is reminiscent of Beckett's novel *Molloy*. Goldberg and McCann also remind us of Beckett's Vladimir and Estragon in *Waiting for Godot*.

Like Rose, Stanley also sees Meg's house as his only refuge, his only security in a hostile world. He has been idle for months, hardly goes out of the house, perhaps because he is too lazy to shave and dress, but perhaps because he is afraid of being recognized, and perhaps because he is afraid of the outside world.

Pinter's characters exist entirely through what they say and do on stage, and this bare existence seems to suffice.

The image of blindness, which we already know from *The Room* and which recurs in a number of Pinter's other plays, is clearly present in *The Birthday Party*. The breaking of Stanley's glasses by McCann thus corresponds to the blinding of Rose in *The Room*.

From the aforesaid, it can be observed that several motifs re-occur in the three plays. First, we have the motif of hunting and pursuit. In *The Dumb Waiter*, the hunt is suspenseful, for the two hunters themselves become the hunted, as they are afraid of what is going on outside the room. In *The Birthday Party*, Stanley is terrified when he learns that the two men are the hunters and he is the hunted. Secondly, the motif of menace, an inseparable part of the Absurd is dominant in the selected plays. Terror is inherent in *The Room* and the play ends on a note of physical violence. In *The Birthday Party*, Stanley fears visitors. In *The Dumb Waiter*, the outside forces menace a questioning killer. Thirdly, the motif of security which is threatened by the modern world receives emphasis in the three plays. Rose talks of how warm the room is, but the cold frightens her. Ben in *The Dumb Waiter* finds his dumbness a guarantee of survival and security. Stanley is secure in his room till the two visitors arrive. The motif of security and the poignant reference to its absence in the modern world, intensifies the experience of the audience/reader in such plays. The selected plays, like the others of Pinter, represent characters 'at the extreme edge of their living. Pinter's plays attempt to translate in dramatic language the "febrile pulsing of an inexpressible terror"[3] which we face in the world.

NOTES

1. Martin Esslin, *The Theatre of the Absurd* (Peregrine, 1987).
2. Harold Pinter, *The Birthday Party* (London: Methuen, 1960).
3. Ronald Hayman, *Harold Pinter* (An H.E.B. paperback, Contemporary Playwright Series, 1975).

"A Play is a Play, is a Play": T.S. Eliot's *Murder in the Cathedral*

V.M. MADGE

One of the chief functions of the syllabus-framing authorities of a University is to ensure that the syllabus they frame is nationally, if not internationally, competitive. Any attempt to fulfil that function is generally met with apprehensive cries of "difficult" not from students but, surprisingly, from teachers themselves. And when the prescription happens to be an Eliot text, such howls of despair and deprecation simply rend the skies. Not surprisingly, therefore, when some years ago, T.S. Eliot's *Murder in the Cathedral* was prescribed in the Modern English Drama Course for B.A. of University of Pune, more and more desperate became the S.O.S.s from teachers and—such are our standards—a most desperate demand for organizing a workshop for teachers to help them put across the text to students, was made. Anybody familiar with our academic ethos will readily see that such a pedagogical 'workshop' is a euphemism for getting the text explained word for word. Accordingly, a workshop was arranged for teachers with a view to enabling them to put *Murder in the Cathedral* across to B.A. students.

Two persons, who, I suspect, had nothing to do with the undergraduates of our University, were the only ones to present their papers. While the papers had nothing relevant in themselves for the purpose of the workshop, they were symptomatic of a view of literary studies that is both misguided and misguiding. Hence this paper.

The first paper argued that as Eliot's political opinions were 'reactionary'—whatever that may mean in the Post-Cold War world—the play was anti-democratic in spirit; that Becket could hardly be considered a saint or a martyr, for, after all, what does he die for? An oligarchical cause of keeping the 'privileges' of the clergy intact; that, to suit his anti-democractic vision, Eliot had 'distorted' history. The second paper arguing on similar lines, condemned the play in more sophisticated terms by calling it 'christian apologetics.' Whatever the difference in their terms of condemnation, the papers shared some common assumptions about the study of literature. For instance, both the paper-readers seemed to suppose that it is quite legitimate to disregard the mode of being of a text and to treat it as something else. Put it simply and more specifically, it seemed quite valid to forget that *Murder in the Cathedral* is a play and not a socio-political or theological tract. But that is precisely how the paper-readers chose to look at the play. In their defence, it could be argued that generic distinctions of writing are no longer on and that everything is now subsumed under the comprehensive Derridean umbrella of 'ecriture.' Had empiricism not been implicitly brushed aside with such brashness as is associated with these and other kindred theoretical stances, it would have been perceived along with Raman Selden in *Criticism and Objectivity* that their extra-ordinary ingenuity notwithstanding, the new theorists have not yet been able to get over the empiricist bind of fact and value. No matter how fuzzy the generic boundaries are, it perhaps can't be helped that some writing is fact-oriented and some value-oriented. A moment's reflection will lead one to see that it was precisely this factor that made Aristotle distinguish between Homer and Empedocles in the very opening chapter of *Poetics.* "Homer has nothing at all in common with Empedocles except the metre. It is just to call Homer a poet, but we must consider Empedocles a physicist than a poet."

In the nineteenth century, De Quincey drew a line of demarcation between Literature of Power and Literature of Knowledge, which still remains valid and, alas, neglected by our formulators of theory. On similar lines, in our own time I.A. Richards made a distinction between statements and pseudo-statements. If these "elements" of our tradition had constituted and formed the critical consciousness of those paper-readers, perhaps they would not have mistaken Eliot's play as history or a theological tract; and seen it for what it is; a poetic play, a work of literary art, that examines deeply the question of Becket's sainthood. By concentrating on the play as a work of art, their eyes would have opened to their otherwise glaring theoretical shortcomings and would have "seen" their own blindness to the textual facts.

The argument that as Eliot's political inclinations were anti-democratic, Becket was no saint, betrays ignorance about the basics of literary studies. First, there is a confusion between the playwright and the protagonist. By no stretch of imagination can Eliot be identified with Becket in such a reductive and totalizing manner. Even assuming that Eliot's opinions were what they are charged to be—a point I have contested in an article of mine—one wonders what they have to do with the story of Becket's martyrdom. Secondly, it is clear that the paper-reader, who obviously is an earnest vigilante about democracy in the world, does not seem to have given a thought to the implications of the argument: in what way does Becket's defeat and consequent triumph of Henry II augur well for the most cherished ideal of democracy? Is it not more useful to look at the play as a story of the conflict between the church and the state both symbolizing at the time "feudalistic" power? Thirdly, and most importantly, the argument raises, in its wake, the old question of poetry and belief which, one thought, Coleridge had settled. To argue that the "ideology" either of an author or the one presented by him in the work, is not acceptable and, therefore, the work is not worth our attention or worth anything cuts at the very root of critical engagement. Such a methodology would rule out, for instance, Shakespeare's tragedies of kings and generals, Dante's *Divine Comedy* or Milton's *Paradise Lost*, for the modern world no longer believes in their world-view. In *Biographia Literaria*, Coleridge shows a solution to such an impasse by his notion of "willing suspension of disbelief which alone constitutes poetic faith."

When asked to cite specific examples of Eliot's distortion of history, the paper-reader was unable to produce any and, in fact, went on to argue that by "distortion" what was meant was that Eliot had given a very selective picture of facts and had, thus, not given us a "complete account" of history. Again when questioned which facts were "omitted" by Eliot, not a single instance was given by the paper-reader. Nor did it come out satisfactorily as to what "a complete account" meant. When is an account "complete"? In this connection, Terry Eagleton's similar attack on George Eliot's *Middlemarch* is worth looking into. Eagleton argued that George Eliot's is a highly selective account of the provincial life during the Victorian period and is, as such, an incomplete historical account. By concentrating on the bourgeois life, George Eliot had left many gaps in the text, therefore what she does not say is far more important than what she does say. Eagleton went on to fill up these textual gaps in the novel by giving facts about proletarian life. The question still remains: what makes Eagleton's account more "complete" rather than George Eliot's? Are they not both selective in their facts? And if selection is inevitable, George Eliot has as much right as Eagleton to choose her facts. In fact, one of the elementary lessons of literary appreciation and evaluation is the recognition that art is after all selection. Even if one chooses to treat a literary work of art as a piece of history—as our paper-reader evidently did—statements from deconstructionists like Derrida should prove enlightening. According to them, to write is to choose. If so, why, then, blame Eliot or, for that matter, any other writer for being selective in his presentation of facts.

In the eighteenth century, Laurence Sterne underscored the inevitable selectivity and hence fictionality of all fiction by his evident inability to carry out Horace's dictum—*ab ovo*—in beginning the autobiographical account of *Tristram Shandy, Esq.* Had the paper-reader even a nodding acquaintance with these commonplaces of literary and critical history, such a methodological mess and misguided argumentation could have been averted. But sometimes, the glamour of theory and ideology proves too dazzling, almost blinding.

The blinding effect of the dazzle of such 'pre'-, more often than not 'mis'-, conceived theoretical positions, leading you to "tedious argument of insidious intent" is seen in the charge, no doubt couched in duly sophisticated diction, of *Murder in the Cathedral* being an instance of "Christian apologetics." A piece of external evidence such as the play being "commissioned" for the annual festival at Canterbury was adduced to prop up this argument. Nothing could be more simplistic than to argue that because Eliot was asked to write a play for the festival, he obliged by writing a duly propagandist work on Becket. In fact the argument is more than simplistic. It is false. For what, then, does one make of the knight's address at the end? Does it not make the text adequately open-ended and the meaning sufficiently indeterminate for our modern tastes? And what about Becket's own comment on how his line of action might appear to some people as the "senseless self-slaughter of a lunatic"— a verdict echoed later on in the play by Richard Brito, the last of the knights to speak. Such post-modernist textual strategies are seen at work in the warning sounded by the Fourth Tempter to Becket regarding the ultimate futility of his martyrdom. To prevent the frontiers between art and apologetics getting further blurred than already done by such a charge, perhaps it may prove useful to compare *Murder in the Cathedral* with Shaw's *Saint Joan* especially with regard to the treatment of the sainthood theme. Whereas the former presents Becket's sainthood from a religious perspective, culminating in Becket's Christmas sermon as well as from the secular viewpoint culminating in the knights' address to the audience, leaving the ultimate choice to the reader/spectator, Shaw, in trying to show that Joan was simply an individual far ahead of her times in certain respects, seems to indulge exactly in the secular rationalist post-mortem explanation of which the Fourth Tempter had warned Becket.

> When miracles cease, and the faithful desert you.
> And men shall only do their best to forget you.
> And later is worse, when men will not hate you
> Enough to defame or to execrate you,
> But pondering the qualities that you lacked
> Will only try to find the historical fact.
> When men shall declare that there was no mystery
> About this man who played a certain part in history.

If anybody is being 'apologetic' it is Shaw, out to spread his Darwinian evolutionary 'gospel,' according to which the burning of Joan as a witch and a heretic and her later canonization are both different forms of misunderstanding. The 'real' Joan is the one presented by Shaw. The reader has no choice. Such ideological im-position is simply absent from *Murder in the Cathedral.* To describe the Eliot-play as 'apologetics' is to ignore its textual and presentational complexity and to indulge in an unseemly game of reductionism all in the name of theoretical sophistication.

Had the play been approached as it came, had enough attention been paid to its mode of being, the workshop would have proved more useful to the teachers. For then, the discussion would have centred around such relevant topics as

1. Eliot's involvement in the revival of poetic drama.
2. Eliot's experimentation with classical drama especially with reference to his use of chorus.
3. The treatment of the themes of sainthood, conflict between the church and the state.
4. The structure of the play with the neat balancing of the Temptation-scene and the Knights' Address that sandwich Becket's Christmas sermon.
5. Imagery and symbolism in the play.
6. The thematic spill from Eliot's poetry into his drama—the theme of time and change etc.

All this should clarify the world of difference between having an open mind and a pre-conceived ideological approach, despite Althusser's redefinition of 'ideology.'

Note: As the papers referred to in this article have not been published so far, only their general line of argument is indicated here. Perhaps, in the circumstances, it can't be helped.

John Osborne's *Look Back in Anger*: A Critique of Welfare State

JAYAPRAKASH A. SHINDE

The Welfare State is the concept of government in which the state plays a key role in the protection and promotion of the economic and social welfare of its citizens. The basic principles of the Welfare State are simple: first, every human being is entitled to a minimum of material well-being, such as food, clothing and decent housing; second, expanding living standards are possible with the existing physical resources and scientific knowledge; and third, the state has the right and duty to act when private initiative fails. Thus it is based on the principles of equality of opportunity, equitable distribution of wealth, and public responsibility for those unable to avail themselves of the minimal provisions for a good life. The realization of these principles is usually attempted in practice through free public education and various forms of social insurance against unemployment, accident, illness, and old age.

This term, which gained general currency after 1945, seems to have originated with William Temple (Archbishop of Canterbury from 1942): "We have . . . seen that in place of the conception of Power State we are led to that of the Welfare State." (*Citizen and Churchman*, 1941) The modern use of the term is associated with the comprehensive measures of social insurance adopted in 1948 by Great Britain on the basis of the *Report on Social Insurance and Allied Services* (1942) by Sir William (later Lord) Beveridge, who is known as the 'father of the Welfare State.' The Report proposed to erect a comprehensive system of social security, making provision for unemployment, sickness, disability, accident, old age, and most other eventualities. It also assumed that a comprehensive health service would be established, available to all. The Report became the foundation upon which the post-war Welfare State was subsequently erected. In the twentieth century, wherever the earlier concept of the passive, *laissez faire* state has been abandoned, almost all states have sought to provide at least some of the measures of social insurance associated with the Welfare State.

Two years laster, Beveridge produced another report, *Full Employment in a Free Society* (1944), in which he showed how the state might regulate the level of economic activity in such a way as to insure full employment. Since unemployment had been the principal curse of the inter-War years, the attention given to the problem was not surprising. What Beveridge sought to achieve with his proposals was full employment in a *free society*. The essential citizen liberties to be preserved under all circumstances are listed by him as follows: "Freedom of worship, speech, writing, study and teaching; freedom of assembly and of association for political and other purposes, including the bringing about of a peacful change of the governing authority; freedom in choice of occupation; and freedom in the management of a personal income." The private ownership of the means of production, Beveridge remarked, might be a good economic device or not, but was "not an essential citizen liberty in Britain, because it is not and never has been enjoyed by more than a very small proportion of the British people." Still, Beveridge thought that full employment could be attained while a community 'held firmly to private enterprise.'[1] And, in the same year, the Government issued its own *Full Employment White Paper* (1944), pledging itself to maintain the level of employment at a high level. A revolution had been accomplished in people's understanding of the potential role of goverment in the economy. Numerous other proposals relating to post-War reconstruction were put forward and so far as education was concerned, plans were actually translated into legislation before the peace. The 1944 Education Act made secondary education free to all and raised the leaving age.

The conception of the Welfare State had a strong appeal also in the United States. Public policy in the United States steadily evolved toward more economic welfare and security. Theodore Roosevelt's Square Deal, Woodrow Wilson's New Freedom, Franklin Roosevelt's New Deal and Harry Truman's Fair Deal were all stages in the extension of welfare for more and more people. The American social scientists examined the issue of the Welfare State from the viewpoints of history, economics, and politics. In the context of American enterprise, Russell W. Davenport preferred using the term "Welfare Capitalism' (*Fortune*, Vol. XL, October 1949). In a forum on "The Democratic Limits of the Welfare State" (*The American Scholar*, Vol. XIX, Autumn 1950), Louis M. Hacker was apprehensive lest the Welfare State threatened technical innovation, fiscal integrity, and individual opportunity by excessive concentration on power; but, by contrast, Max Lerner viewed the Welfare State as 'but a preliminary stage of full-fledged socialism' and saw in all modern states in the West the determined effort to obtain the maximum welfare from a combination of both, the private and the public, forms of enterprise. Arnold J. Toynbee argued in *The New York Times Magazine* (October 21, 1951): "Our age will be remembered chiefly neither for its horrifying crimes nor for its astonishing inventions, but for its having been the first age since the dawn of civilization, some five or six thousand years back, in which people dared to think it practicable to make the benefits of civilization available for the whole human race."

The Welfare State in an even more thorough-going form, with state aid for the individual in almost all phases of his life—'from the cradle to the grave'—is exemplified in the Netherlands and the social democratic governments of Western Europe. The concept is almost an article of faith in the new states of Asia and Africa.

II

Simultaneously with the conduct of a desperate war, the British coalition government in the years from 1940 to 1945 laid plans to ensure that when the war ended, there should be no repetition of the widespread unemployment that had dogged the nation in the 1920s and 1930s. World War II had been the people's war; the nation's rulers, whether they liked it or not, had to depend on the willing co-operation of the ruled, including even scorned and underprivileged section of society, manual workers and women. This co-operation must be paid for by concessions in the direction of a standard of living for the poor, greater social activity and improved welfare services. 'Social Security' became a familiar term denoting the various national services that were to bring in the Welfare State with its ideal of 'fair share for all.'

The sweeping victory at the general election in 1945 enabled the Labour Party to implement hurriedly its nationlization programme for the power-supply, transport and other industries, and to establish National Health Service. Almost overnight, Britain found itself an affluent state in which full employment, high wages, family allowances and other public benefits appeared to promise a Utopia for millions. It had been assumed that the removal of economic stresses would bring contentment to the majority, but the experience of the following decades did not justify the expectation. In the process of solving the problem of unemployment through public policies aiming at full employment, new problems developed which were not anticipated before, and of which Beveridge seemed to have no idea when he wrote *Full Employment in a Free Society*. The state was found as uncongenial and unsympathetic a master as many private employers had been.

As the natural result of the impact of World War II, the English society divided into two worlds, one of those who did not believe that anything had changed and continued to act as if nothing had changed, and the other of those, generally the younger generation, who not only recognized change, but welcomed it. The victory of Clement Attlee's Labour Party represented the victory of the younger intelligentsia supporting the traditional working-class vote. This division widened further. The new generation rejected tradition and laughed at the old generation. Banham elaborates: "Both sides had their strongholds. The one could nationalise industry, give away colonies, create opportunities for free education to the highest levels. . . . But the other could hang on to what it had in a stubborn exercise in self-perpetuation of the top jobs, could still use the residual wealth and potential and social power to maintain its exclusiveness, and could still insinuate its standards into the morality of the society." He adds further: "Osborne writes from the experiences and the frustrations of the new generation."[2]

A mood of sullen discontent settled upon large numbers of those whom the new order had been designed to benefit. Crime and prostitution, which were till now believed to be by-products of property, flourished as never before. Those to whom much was given now desired more. Increased educational opportunities up to university level bred a body of young men and women culturally severed from their families and socially rootless. Finding that a university degree did not of itself admit them to a well-rewarded profession, some tended to fall back upon the illusion that the world owed them an effortless living. Such 'anti-heroes' as Dixon in Kingsley Amis's *Lucky Jim* (1954) and Porter in John Osborne's *Look Back in Anger* (1956) represent the Angry Young Man of the 1950s who strongly believed that they were harshly treated by the world of their time.

III

John Osborne's *Look Back in Anger* is set in a one-room flat in a Midland town, the 'home' of James Porter and his wife Alison. James is always called 'Jimmy' in the play, which according to A.C. Ward is "a symptom of a curious form of inverted snobbery, rooted in the habit of the period, whereby a peculiarly democratic virtue was assumed to lie in the diminutives of first names, so that William became a more acceptable 'comrade' if called Bill."[3] Banham explains the significance of the setting: "The audience was invited to look into a world that was singularly sordid, but very real. Gas stove, chest of drawers littered with clothing, books etc., light from a skylight, the hero slouched in an old arm-chair reading a paper, the heroine ironing in the middle of the room dressed in one of her husband's old shirts." (12) The play represented a revolution in the content of a play. English people were unfamiliar with what appeared in *Look Back in Anger.* To most people the setting was a challenge to their sensitivity and the content a challenge to their trust in the Welfare State. The play is occupied mostly by the long tirades of abuse which Jimmy aims at his society, its absence of values and its hypocrisy. Much of this abuse spills over on his friend Cliff and his wife Alison in the form of pinching and bitterly humorous attacks. Jimmy hates Alison for her origins, higher than his own; he regards Cliff, uneducated but with 'natural intelligence of the self-taught,' as inferior to him. And he is infuriated with his society just because, though a university graduate, he can find nothing better to do than keep a sweet stall in a local market. Frederick Lumley upholds Jimmy's angry outbursts of abuse as "a return to the directness of language long absent."[4]

John Osborne's description of Jimmy in the opening stage directions establishes him at once as an Angry Young Man, an anti-hero: "Jimmy is a tall, thin young man about twenty-five, wearing a very worn tweed jacket and flannels. Clouds of smoke fill the room from the pipe he is smoking. He is a disconcerting mixture of sincerity and cheerful malice, of tenderness and freebooting cruelty; restless, importunate, full of pride, a combination which alienates the sensitive and insensitive alike. Blistering honesty, or apparent honesty, like his, makes few friends. To many he may seem sensitive to the point of vulgarity. To others, he is simply a loudmouth. To be as vehement as he is to be almost non-commital."[5] Cliff is presented as 'a soothing, natural counterpoint to Jimmy': "If Jimmy alienates love, Cliff seems to exact it."

Simon Trussler presents quite a convincing interpretation of the title of the play in the context of the character of Jimmy: "He looks back in anger only because he looks back in nostalgia; and his compulsive verbosity is a protective device, an armoury of words with which an easily-wounded man defends himself against those who best recognize his vulnerability."[6] The roots of Jimmy's anger lie in the past—in his father's premature, lingering death and his mother's inadequate middle-class compromises. He directs his anger, intensified further with his own disillusionment, to Alison. He attacks her with all the fury of his passion. He hates her for her middle-class upbringing. He wants her to surrender after suffering and humiliation. Jimmy regards Alison's toleration of him on a par with the patronage with which society has given him education and then denied him an effective role, reserving that for its aristocrats. Unable to wage an active war against the society which he believes as wholly responsible for his failure, he seems to take unsavoury pleasure in torturing his wife with abuse.

After Alison leaves him and goes with her father, Jimmy lives with her friend Helena. This change does not mean anything to

Jimmy. He always feels that he is living in a world of enemies which does not suit him at all. His general enemies are those he sees as smug, privileged, and worsely those who are successful. Ailson's brother Nigel is such an enemy. Jimmy attacks the Conservative Party, its candidates and supporters, politicians in general, the regular army, its officers and the public schools. At an early age, when his father died, he had learnt 'what it was to be angry—angry and helpless.' His anger is always linked with his helplessness—helplessness in the face of death and failure. He thinks himself incapable of achieving success and blames the vicious world for this. He rails against his society, against everyone in his society. Griffiths sees Jimmy as "a wheel spinning fruitlessly in the mud, flinging it purposelessly in the face of anyone who comes near and then crying out in terror at the thought of being left alone in the dark."[7] Jimmy thinks of himself as an 'objectionable young man.' He wants to be heard. His demand to be heard is a reflection of his desire to be needed. As Osborne says, "Jimmy alienates love"; and yet, he is loved, by Alison, by Helena and by Cliff. In the last Act, Alison returns; she has lost her baby; she is reduced to despair. Helena leaves to allow the couple to continue the relationship which only fantasizing against the dreadful reality can sustain. At the close of the play, Jimmy and Alison are left clinging together, Jimmy saying, 'with a kind of mocking, tender irony': "We'll be together in our bear's cave, and our squirrel's drey, and we'll live on honey and nuts—lots and lots of nuts. And we'll sing songs about ourselves—about warm trees and snug caves, and lying in the sun." (96)

John Osborne presents Jimmy Porter in *Look Back in Anger* as an Angry Young Man who was disillusioned, because the Welfare State did not offer him a life suitable for his talents, because the changing society in which he believed was, in reality, as stagnant and class-dominated as ever. The play opens with discontent and fury and ends in resigned despair, suggesting that the Welfare State had failed in fulfilling the promise of good life and that, on the contrary, the majority was subjected to discontent, fury and inevitable despair. Osborne shows Jimmy as a misfit in this world and obviously his experiences were widely shared by the majority of the young men of the 1950s. The only way to get reconciled with the disheartening situation around was, Osborne seems to suggest, to have recourse to the world of fantasy.

NOTES

1. William Ebenstein, *Modern Political Thought: The Great Issues* (2nd Edition, New Delhi: Oxford & IBH, 1947, Indian Edition, 1970), p. 676.
2. M. Banham, *Osborne* (Edinburgh: Oliver and Boyd, 1969), p. 15.
3. A.C. Ward, *Twentieth Century English Literature* (London: The English Language Book Society and Methuen, 1964), p. 140.
4. Frederick Lumley, *New Trends in 20th Century Drama* (London: Barrie and Rockliff, 1967), p. 222.
5. John Osborne, *Look Back in Anger* (London: Faber and Faber, 1957), pp. 9-10.
6. Simon Trussler, *John Osborne* (London: Longmans, Green, 1969), p. 11.
7. Gareth Griffiths, *John Osborne: Look Back in Anger* (York Notes, Longman York Press, 1981), p. 57.

A Man for All Seasons as Robert Bolt's Diagnosis of the Modern Man's Malady

SUNANDA P. CHAVAN

As the subtitle of Robert Bolt's play clarifies, *A Man for All Seasons*[1] (1960) is a play of Sir Thomas More, a Christian saint put to death by Henry VIII in 1532. Bolt is one of those modern dramatists who exploit thematic potentialities of history of saints to diagnose the modern man's malady. Living in the post-war decades of disillusionment with rationalism on the one hand, and with culture on the other, Bolt seeks to define the modern man against the background of Sir Thomas More.

Bolt's 'Preface' may be accepted as a part of his play in which he is anxious to offer possible perspectives for the interpretation of his play. He explains in it the causes of his fascination for the hero. The modern man and his society suffer from a deep sense of non-identity. As Bolt puts it, 'we no longer have, as past societies have had, any picture of individual Man . . . by which to recognize ourselves and against which to measure ourselves; we are anything. But if anything, then nothing . . . it is our true present position.' (p. xi) The impotence of society to help the individual to gain a sense of identity is exposed further by the dramatist in his statement, 'the individual who tries to plot his position by reference to our society finds no fixed points, but only the vaunted absence of them.' (xi) Through his choice of Sir Thomas More, Bolt illustrates 'individual man,' a 'fixed' point by which we recognize our negative selves.

The play is, in fact, one of the ways in which the dramatist tries to measure the modern man's tragic lack of what Sir Thomas

More stands for. Bolt calls More 'the hero of selfhood.' The modern man's malady is the absence of 'self.' The play is his attempt to do what he expects 'men of science, thinkers, artists' to do. He wants them 'to get for us—a sense of selfhood without resort to magic.' (xiv) It is the play of 'self' for the 'non-self' age.

The concept of 'self' as Bolt understands it, is allowed to shape gradually through the conflict between Sir Thomas More and the King. More's refusal to give his opinion on the problem of the King's divorce is sarcastically referred to, by Wolsey the Chancellor, at the beginning of the play as More's 'moral squint.' It is, no doubt, identified with the more familiar concept of one's own 'conscience,' throughout the play. Wolsey represents the common view, which is later corroborated by Henry, that conscience is a private matter and should not be allowed to interfere with one's duties towards the state. More believes such an attitude to be disastrous for the state. If welfare of the state is the purpose of statesmanship, the purpose is itself defeated if the statesman is not guided by his conscience—his sense of right and wrong—in the matters of the state. He answers Wolsey, 'when statesmen forsake their own private conscience for the sake of their public duties . . . they lead their country by a short route to chaos.' (12)

Loyalty to 'self' or to 'conscience' is the vital need of life in the case of More. Hence, he reacts passionately against Roper's warm appreciation of his act of resignation as a noble 'gesture.' It suggests 'morality' to be an exhibitionistic act of an individual strongly manipulated to impress his society. For More, loyalty to conscience cannot be a strategy. It is, in itself, a way of life. To be moral is to live according to morals and that is being practical. He cannot think of life in which morality is restricted to theory only. Hence his indignant answer to Roper, 'Oh, now I understand you, till morality's not practical morality is a gesture.' (56)

Faced with the conflicting loyalties to the King and the conscience, More prefers to be loyal to his conscience than to any other thing. It encourages Cromwell to accuse him of 'self-conceit' against him. However, More is humble and honest in pointing out the difference between self-conceit and self-respect the one being a luxury, the other being a condition of life. He argues that it is 'pure necessity for respect of my soul.' When Cromwell suggests his so-called concept of respect for his soul to be nothing but pride of self and hence self-centredness of a proud man, More wants him to understand that 'a man's soul is his self'—the essential identity of an individual. It is the bond between man and god—the creator and the creation—and, hence, the only justification for man's existence on the earth. He clarifies this metaphysical dimension of 'self' when he asks Norfolk after forfeiting his property, 'And when we stand before God, and you are sent to paradise for doing according to your conscience and I am damned for not doing according to mine, will you come with me, for fellowship?' (78)

Significantly enough, More does not regard his conscience as the criterion for assessing others around him. He is steadfast in his own view of the King's act, but is not interested in offering judgement over others. He regards severance of the Church of England from the Church of Rome as sin, but says, at the same time, 'what matters to me is not whether it's true or not but that I believe it to be true, or rather not that I *believe* it, but *I* believe it.' (53) Even on the threshold of death, he does not want to blame others who support the King, because of the simple reason, 'I have no window to look into other man's conscience, I condemn no one.'

Bolt here appears not to emphasize the religious integrity of More as seen in his belief in the Church of Rome. His approach is humanistic rather than religious or spiritual. It does not matter what More believes, what matters is that he believes it with the steadfastness not found among others. The whole problem is rightly pinpointed by Cromwell when he tells Rich, "well, there are those men who—you know—'upright,' 'steadfast,' men who want themselves to be the constant factor in the situation." (45) More argues with Margaret, who wants him to submit, as the only reasonable course of action, 'since (in fact) we see that avarice, anger, envy, pride, sloth, lust and stupidity commonly profit far beyond humility, chastity, fortitude, justice, and thought, and have to choose, to be human at all—why then perhaps we must stand fast a little—over at the risk of being heroes.' (84)

The only alternative to honesty to self is spiritual death. Hence, More refuses to take an oath although it is the only means by which he can escape the punishment of death. He tells his daughter 'when a man is taking oath, Meg, he's holding his own self in his own hands. Like water and if he opens his fingers then he needn't hope to find himself again.' (83) As he tells Rich before going to his own death, 'it profits a man nothing to give his soul for the whole world.' (95) Commitment to self is rationally inexplicable because it is not, as he tells, 'a matter of reason, finally it's the matter of love.'

What establishes a point of contact between More and the modern man is his ordinariness in spite of extraordinariness. Robert Bolt quotes Robert Whittinton on the title page describing More thus, 'where is the man of that gentleness, loveliness and affability? And as time requireth a man of marvellous mirth and pastimes, and sometimes of as sad gravity a man for all seasons.' He is a perfectly normal man interested in the taste of wine and of Burgundy which, he regrets, Roper cannot enjoy. He loves custard made by his wife and can appreciate her dress. He is healthy enough to share a joke about the 'simple' supper prepared by Alice for the King. He can balance perfectly his need of secrecy to avoid danger as a Chancellor with his deep love for his wife in playfully evasive answer to her anxious enquiries.

More is ordinary in spite of his saintliness primarily because he fears death. He does not romanticize it. When Chapuys flatters him by calling him as 'the English Socrates,' he tells him very clearly that he has 'no taste for hemlock.' (49) He is so eager to meet his family in the prison after a year's solitary confinement that he does not hesitate to push Roper towards the Jailer in order to keep him engaged in talk so that he may get more time to speak. He struggles hectically to defend himself from punishment to the last moment by using his talent as a lawyer. He is not ashamed to accept his inability to answer even a man like Rich. More says, 'I'd give the Devil benefit of law, for my own safety's sake.'

More thinks, though wrongly, that his silence will protect him under law. Even before the final crisis, he makes it perfectly clear to his daughter, that their 'natural business lies in escaping.' (74) When he is reconciled to the inevitability of his punishment of death, he is all the more anxious to protect his family from sinister doom in near future. Hence, he advises them to leave the country by 'different boats from different ports.'

A Man for All Seasons is a play of Conscience versus Convenience, or of idealistic versus practical approach to life. There is conflict between Sir Thomas More who stands for Conscience, and the King, his men and the members of More's own family who stand for Convenience. On the most obvious level, it is the conflict between Sir Thomas More and the King—a statesman and his political head. The men like Wolsey, Cromwell, Rich, Duke of Norfolk and Cranmer have been loyal to the King and his desires; even Chapuys, the Spanish ambassador joins hands with Cromwell at the end. Conscience and Convenience are two ways of life. Conscience is a condition for living which demands unwavering sense of commitment to one's own self at the cost of every other commitment in life. Convenience involves sacrifice of the self. It is the key to success in practical life and a strategy to keep trouble away—the most popular philosophy of life for ages and especially chosen by the present generation, according to Bolt. Cromwell regards Convenience as the constant factor and thinks that, 'the normal aim of administration is to keep steady, this factor of convenience.' (43) Convenience is the safest policy of life for ordinary people in society because it is the most useful. The aim of convenience is to live, the aim of conscience is to live meaningfully. The conflict between the two develops as conflict between individual and society because only a few individuals over ages have courage to live a life of conscience. The society always prefers to live by convenience.

The dramatist offers many forms of conscience through different characters. Like More, the King is also described as a man of conscience, but his conscience is convenience masked. He forces Pope earlier to sanction marriage between himself and his brother's wife in spite of the Biblical opposition. When it becomes inconvenient to live with Catherine because he loves Anne, the King is now anxious that Pope should change his earlier consent and declare such marriage to be sin. The conflict between the King and More is a conflict within the King—his desire to marry Anne and his conscience that prevents him from it. More is the voice of Henry's inner conscience which cannot shake off a feeling of guilt for what he does. As he tells More during his visit to More's house, he admires More, because he is honest, truthful and sincere. He tells More, 'though we love praise, yet we love truth better.' (33)

More resigns from his post as the Lord Chancellor when the Church of England declares itself independent of the Church of Rome. His views then cease to be that of 'administrative inconvenience.' Yet the King's guilty conscience seeks More's total destruction because his inner voice of conscience cannot be silenced until More is put to death. The very silence of More becomes, for the King, a protest against his life of convenience.

The conflict between Conscience and Convenience is a conflict between the changeless and the ever-shifting. Rich changes conveniently from being More's friend to being a witness against him when he is bribed with the post of Attorney General for Wales. Norfolk changes from being friend to being a member of His Majesty's Council appointed to enquire the charges against More because he fears punishment from the King for his friendship with More. Even Chapuys joins Cromwell in ridiculing More for his foolish act of accepting death rather than submitting his conscience to the desires of the King.

Common Man is the most significant character in the play both from thematic and structural points of view. As Bolt states in the Preface, 'he represents what is common to us all.' (xviii) He is the greatest worshipper of the God of Convenience and confesses that 'it is better a live rat than a dead lion.' In the role of steward, he accepts his inability to understand the man like More but refuses most practically to serve him, when More resigns his post. He exploits his former position of being More's steward, and sells bits of information about him to all who require it—Cromwell, Rich, Chapuys—as long as they pay him for it. He is the very opposite of More in his lack of conscience and the choice of convenience. He hates Rich yet succeeds in being his steward through sheer flattery after he rises to high position. His willingness to take oath is a parody of More's anxiety not to take oath. The only lesson he learns and wants the audience to learn at the end in 'Alternative Ending' is 'just don't make trouble or if you must make trouble, make the sort of trouble that's expected.' (100)

Structurally, the introoduction of Common Man aims at 'alienation effect,' as Bolt says in the preface. The style used is, as he explains, 'a bastardized version of the one most associated with Brecht.' (xvii) Brecht introduces a dramatic form in which the audience is prevented from suspension of disbelief. A play is not 'illusion of reality' demanding total involvement of the audience with the action. He develops methods of writing, producing and acting which embody a critical detachment of the audience from the action of the play. The illusion is deliberately fractured and alienation effect is produced, to enable the audience to enter the role of a critic and assess the situation at each stage of development of action. Bolt's Common Man is, at once, the character inside the play and a critic outside it. His commentary establishes a link between the historical world of the play and the contemporary world of the audience. He is not only a strategy in the design to join the scenes but more significantly, the protagonist of the practical view of life which complements the spiritual in More. Together, Common Man and More complete life's vision. Bolt also follows Brecht's epic theatre form in giving his play a loosely episodic plot. He chooses crucial episodes like Wolsey's death and More's appointment in his place, the Act of Parliament to sever the Church of England from the Church of Rome, the life-imprisonment of More, and his final death. But the dramatist is not tempted to exploit them for their emotional potential because the play focuses on More's struggle to follow conscience. The apparently romantic event of marriage between Roper and Margaret is bypassed to concentrate on the event of More's attack against Roper for his heretic views. Even the tragic death of More is treated by Bolt not as tragedy but the divine comedy of conscience. More cannot be defeated because his death is merely bodily death, the spirit remains invincible.

The dramatist introduces passages from history within the play to intensify 'alienation effect' and counter-balance the possible sentimental effect. Cromwell's crude method used against More with the help of Norfolk and Rich might produce pity for the hero. But a passage from history already informs how Cromwell, Norfolk, Rich and the King himself ended. Those who conspire to punish the innocence are blind to their own punishments awaiting them in future. Thus the audience is prevented from emotional involvement with More and encouraged to assess the journey of selfhood, objectively.

More's triple conflict focuses on man's relationship with society as an individual, his relationship with family, and his relationship with himself. The ambitious politicians like Cromwell, Norfolk and Rich use convenience for achieving power, position and money. On the other hand, the members of More's family are forced to be on the side of convenience because of their desire for safety, both for them and for him. They admire his courage to stand by conscience but they fear its consequences for his and their sake. They do not succeed in converting the idealist to the practical way of life, but they are sensitive enough to realize his nobility. More's adamant refusal to submit to the King's desires forces them into a life of poverty, but his supreme moral courage in facing its tragic consequences makes them proud of him. There is an only occasion on which More's loyalty to his self appears to have momentarily weakened—the occasion of his meeting with his wife when he is in prison. Bolt is at his best in this only emotional scene in the play which shows the transformation of Alice. When she sees him after a long interval of a year, she does not embrace him as is done by Margaret but sits at a distance, full of bitterness against the unyielding, obstinate man. She is angry with him for forcing the family into poverty for the sake of his conscience even when he is threatened with death. More tries to be light, then pleads with her, then is overcome with a sense of defeat when she refuses to respond to his pleading. But, at the last moment, she bursts into a loving response. It solaces and gratifies him, and gives him courage to go to death happily and peacefully.

Bolt's More is, as he confesses, different from the historical More. It is a Christian saint appropriated to the writer's purposes. Yet Anthony Kenny, the biographer of Sir Thomas More, thinks that 'the More of Bolt's play turns out to be a less consistent character than the real More, because More's conscience makes him so unbending against the King's laws on the one hand, and so anxious to comply with others, on the other. The apparent inconsistency arises out of More's struggle to achieve a satisfying adjustment between the ideal and the practical approach to the King's marriage. In fact, the play is itself the result of a struggle on the part of the dramatist to search for a possible cure for modern man's malady of life of convenient practicalities which reduce him to non-identity.

NOTES

1. Robert Bolt, *A Man for All Seasons* (Arnold-Heinemann, 1960; 1968).
2. Anthony Kenny, *Thomas More* (Oxford, New York: Oxford University Press, 1983), p. 96.